Peter Ampe
Emily Rammant

# Great Minds Think Unalike

## The Benefits of ADHD, Autism, Dyslexia and OCD

Lannoo

My difference
is my talent

# Who is this book for?

This book is for anyone who may be facing difficulties or uncertainties in life and is struggling to identify the root cause of this unease. You might feel socially awkward in group situations, have zero interest in the school curriculum, or have colleagues who question your unconventional thinking and behaviour. Perhaps you're somewhere on the spectrum of a neurodivergent condition without even realizing it. That might be a shock, but this book shows that a realization like this can come as a relief, even a revelation. A lot of things will suddenly become clear. Things about yourself. About your environment. And you'll also get to know the strengths associated with your atypical brain. In other words, your difference points the way to your talent.

This book will also be of interest to business leaders and HR managers keen to promote greater awareness and appreciation of neurodivergent profiles in the workplace.

# Welcome to the spectrum

Drawing on personal experience, we aim to show that neuropsychological conditions such as AD(H)D (attention-deficit (hyperactivity) disorder), ASD (autism spectrum disorder), dyslexia and OCD (obsessive-compulsive disorder) can also have a positive side. Our aim in this book is not to emphasise the downsides of these conditions, but to highlight the upsides.

Our target audience includes individuals with a diagnosis of AD(H)D, ASD, dyslexia, and/or OCD who have average or above-average intelligence. However, as mentioned in the first paragraph, this book aims to go a step further. We also wrote it for anyone who doesn't have a diagnosis (yet) but does have enough symptoms of a neuropsychological condition to benefit from the special powers that are associated with it. Our approach is based on the observation that all of the above conditions lie on a spectrum. There's nothing binary about neuropsychological conditions. This is very different from, for example, a pregnancy test, which gives either a positive or negative result. In other words, you cannot be a little bit pregnant, but you can have a little bit of ADHD or exhibit some compulsive obsessive behaviour.

Maybe, without realizing it yourself, you lie somewhere on one of these spectrums. That might explain why you've been running up against certain things or hearing certain comments from friends or colleagues all your life. Maybe it also shows the path to your talent and the environment in which you thrive best.

This is not an academic textbook. But we do want to take a fresh look at where the boundary lies between the normal and the atypical brain, and – above all – at the possibilities that this fresh look opens up. But as facts are more convincing and correct data remain important, we have had this book reviewed in its entirety by Theo Compernolle, medical doctor, neuropsychiatrist and former professor.

## I = we

This book is written in the name of Peter Ampe because it started out as my personal confession. But due to my ADHD I was never able to finish it. For that I needed my wife Emily Rammant, whose touch of OCD means she hates to see things left unfinished. Thanks to Emily, existing chapters have been reworked and new chapters and testimonies added. So although you'll read 'I' throughout, know that it always means 'we'.

# Contents

# Confessions of the author

## Short attention span

*'Smells on all sides, bunched together. Each street different smell. Each person too. Then the spring, the summer: smells. Tastes? They say you can't taste wines with your eyes shut or a cold in the head.'* – James Joyce, Ulysses

Starting a book with a reference to James Joyce's novel *Ulysses* is never a good idea. While many people are familiar with the title, very few have actually read the book because it's so difficult to follow.

Maybe you frowned too when you read the first few sentences of this introduction. You're not the only one for whom Joyce's literary ramblings are such a struggle. This is because the author experiments with a narrative technique known as stream of consciousness or internal monologue. Joyce employs this technique to illustrate the myriad thoughts and feelings running through the narrator's mind. They cause the protagonist to jump from topic to topic without warning. Hard to read. But also hard to live with. Because this stream of consciousness is the lived experience of every person with ADHD, but on a much higher level. It's all very poetic to talk about a stream of ideas, while your neurons feel more like a troupe of hyperactive fleas trampolining on a ratty old sofa.

That snap, crackle and pop of distracting thoughts is why it took so long to write this book. I started it in 2016, and I started it again in 2019. In between, I picked up the thread several times, but usually put it down again just as quickly. Sustaining an effort is difficult for me. For example, the fireworks in my head have made me start writing a new introduction several times already, each time with a new angle. Needless to say, that keeps you busy.

Until the summer of 2021, when my wife suggested we form a writing partnership and start to take this book seriously. She brought structure to my ideas, came up with new angles and made sure the book continued to take shape. She does the same in my life, come to think of it.

# I'm not creative

*Istanbul, March 2019.* At the offices of Turkish communications agency 1492Grey, the top creative minds of the Grey Advertising Network are holding a meeting. During this Global Council, as they call this annual creative get-together, the standout campaigns from every office around the world are discussed. The best work is shortlisted for submission to the International Festival of Creativity in Cannes. This is our industry's most important festival – so important, it influences the stock market listings of the networks taking part.

As a new face, tradition requires me to introduce myself informally to the group. Not in a LinkedIn way, but in a Facebook way. The more private things you share, the better the social cohesion afterwards: that's the idea behind it. I decide to introduce myself based on my differences: I confess to being left-handed, colour-blind, afraid of the dark, scarily analytical, with a good memory and an extreme eye for detail. Each difference is illustrated by an anecdote from my childhood. I end my introduction with the one-liner: 'I'm not creative, I just have a couple of deviations.'

My creative colleagues welcome this sign-off with a burst of laughter. It sounds almost like a collective sigh of relief. My words have clearly struck a nerve. Returning to my seat, I decide to take a closer look at everyone in the room. I watch how they behave, how they talk, how they interact with the group. All amazing people, all smart people, but each with their own quirk. Some leap up from their seats every few minutes and start pacing nervously. Maybe a touch of ADHD? Others try to hog the floor the whole time and it's a struggle to get them to shut up. A bit more ADHD in the room? Some inject a rigid logic into every idea and make themselves scarce during the breaks. Isolation-seeking specific to the autism spectrum? Still others insist on their own rituals, even though the group's agenda doesn't really have space for them. Compulsive behaviour?

## Afraid of the dark

I think it was that day that the seed was sown for this book. After a day in the presence of these creative directors, I could almost guess their neurodivergent traits based on the way they functioned. And each of those traits makes them better at what they do. Each one of them differs from the norm, but that's partly why they're so good at their jobs.

Most of them probably saw their own way of thinking and interacting as entirely normal or, in psychological terms, *neurotypical*. Incidentally, I don't have an official diagnosis of neurodivergence myself, though it's apparent to everyone around me. And I've never taken an official test, simply because it wasn't a common thing to do when I was at school. Back then there was no talk of ADHD or ASD and no allowances were made, even for more obvious things such as colour blindness. I found this out for myself the hard way in my first year of school. I can still see myself sitting in the third row, somewhere in the middle. The teacher came up behind me and wondered aloud why I hadn't copied down the title on the board. 'But sir,' I defended myself, 'there isn't a title on the board.' This subversive behaviour earned me a smack around the ear. Which I didn't understand, because I didn't see a title. Red chalk on a green board was completely invisible to me. A few years later, I was sent out of class during a French lesson because I hadn't translated the red text, as asked, but the green text. The teacher saw this as an act of rebellion. That in itself I can understand, because contrariness is in my nature. But mostly I rebel over more important issues.

In short, not everyone welcomed my differences as positive. Though there was also a nursery teacher who – long before anyone realized I was colourblind – told my mother with a degree of pride: 'Mrs Ampe, I think your son will be very creative because he draws green trees with brown leaves.' To some I was rebellious, to others creative. In both cases, however, I was simply colour-blind.

By the way, it wasn't just my unusual perception of colours that got me labelled as creative. People around me also noticed very early on that I look at the world differently. That comes partly from necessity, because I'm left-handed. Try signing something in a bank where the pen is attached to the right-hand side of the counter by a chain that is far too short. You might keep trying in vain to stretch the metal, but eventually you'll need a creative intervention if you're to sign anything. Either you adapt your signature into a vertical version or you adapt the sheet of paper with a spot of origami. This is creativity out of necessity. It provides constant training for your fluid intelligence, the type of intelligence that is good at flexible thinking and problem solving.

But maybe there's more to it. Nowadays I'd surely be diagnosed with ASD. I also have distinct traits of ADHD, anxiety disorders or maybe a very mild form of dyslexia. But ASD for sure. It was through my son, who was diagnosed with ASD, that I suddenly realized that I too may have some form of autism. During the testing leading up to his diagnosis, my wife forwarded a list of ASD symptoms to me. Without explanation. After the first paragraph, I'd read enough. I recognized so much of myself that it was almost funny: a strong feel for language, good at word jokes, extreme eye for detail, visual thinking, highly developed long-term memory, hypersensitivity to stimuli and insensitivity to the emotions of others. The latter in particular has haunted me for quite a while, since it's something I haven't been able to place for a long time.

My suspicion was promptly confirmed by multiple online tests, which, although indicative, left no room for misunderstanding. It was clear that I have quite a few autistic traits. This insight was also liberating, because it suddenly explained the origins of my different perspective on things, my creativity, my difficulty with social contact. It was also reassuring, because I realized that my creativity wasn't dependent on external stimuli. It's simply a permanent condition.

And that permanent condition ties in with my fears and anxieties. Fear of the dark, for example. This is a common childhood fear, but in my case, it persisted into adulthood. Even as a teenager, I slept with the lights on. It wasn't until I lived in a student hall that I realized I had a very active imagination. This self-analysis was prompted by a lecture by the late Etienne

Vermeersch, a Belgian philosopher, ethicist, professor and vice-rector at Ghent University who ascribed the emergence of religions to the human imagination. Why are you afraid in a forest? Because something could be lurking behind every tree. That is the power of imagination.

Since then, I've learned to embrace darkness as a methodology for creative thinking. I only have to catch a snippet of conversation or hear a newsreader's opening words and I promptly think up a whole story of my own. Give me 10% and I'll fill in the other 90%. Darkness in this sense is a metaphor for a minimum amount of information. Just enough to stimulate your imagination and spark ideas. This is why I find the black-and-white images of photographer Dirk Braeckman so intriguing. It's like looking into a dark room. As your eyes get used to the light, you discover more and more. And the things you can't make out, you invent.

Becoming aware of my differences ultimately confirmed that I am working in the right industry, because the communications world needs creativity. This just happens to be what I do every day as an advertising creative on the agency side: find creative solutions to the challenges facing brands. And – this is great for people with ASD – you don't always have to work with others; there are many things you can do on your own.

## Accept your difference, find your talent

While reading this book, you may come to realize that you too are closer to a particular condition than you initially thought. If you already have a diagnosis, you may find it easier to focus on the positives. Always assuming, of course, that the condition is mild enough to not significantly hinder your professional performance. We certainly don't want to minimize the difficulties that can come with neurodivergence. But there's no shortage of books about those. That's why we mainly aim to highlight the other side, the positive side.

It's a law of nature: for every negative, a positive. Neurodivergence comes with cognitive differences from the norm, and that goes both ways. There can be outliers in a good sense, as well as in a bad sense. Professor Amanda Kirby talks about a 'spiky' profile or peak profile because there are peak and valley features. In the example on the next page you can find the profile of a neurotypical person on top and the peak profile of a neurodivergent person below, where certain traits are overdeveloped and others underdeveloped.

This book invites you to explore and chart your differences. The next step is to accept your difference and, yes, even embrace it. We will help you identify what makes you different and reframe it as a talent. Then, using that talent, you will hopefully find a vocation where you can not only make a difference but also find fulfilment. By taking this unusual route, we invite you to use your difference to discover your strengths, and then apply them in order to map out your ideal career path. Still too many people spend a lifetime searching for what they're good at and the environment they can thrive in. While all the time they're simply great minds who think unalike.

## Neurotypical cognitive profile

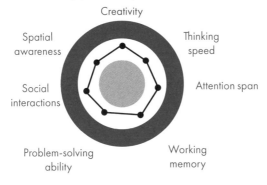

Creativity

Spatial awareness

Thinking speed

Social interactions

Attention span

Problem-solving ability

Working memory

## Neurodivergent cognitive profile

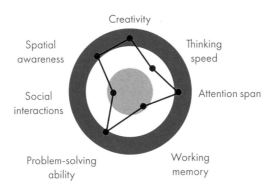

Creativity

Spatial awareness

Thinking speed

Social interactions

Attention span

Problem-solving ability

Working memory

## Accepting

**Learning to live with
your difference**

→ Reconciled

→ Resigned

→ Passive

## Rejecting

**Not accepting
your difference**

→ Denial

→ Angry, anxious

→ Depressed

→ Bitter

# SATISFACTION
# SUCCESS
# HAPPINESS

## Transcending

**Using the talent
of your atypical brain**

→ Appreciation

→ Gratitude

→ Integration

## Improving

**Making the best
of your atypical
brain by training
and compensating**

→ Ambitious

→ Challenged

→ Open to experiment

**Develop the talent
you have,
not the talent you want**

John C. Maxwell

# PART I

# Welcome to the spectrum

# Chapter 1
# On the left of the spectrum

Books on neurodivergence mainly offer coping mechanisms to help people handle their condition better and live as normal a life as possible. Unfortunately, they often forget to stress that there are also positive features associated with neurodivergence.

In 2018, Greta Thunberg told the TEDx conference in Stockholm that she had been diagnosed with obsessive-compulsive disorder and Asperger syndrome (a form of ASD associated with high IQ). She ascribed the doggedness of her commitment partly to her autism. It makes it much easier for her to be, in her own words, 'laser sharp' and to say bluntly what she thinks. In other words, she can make purely rational statements without any sense of the social consequences. Only someone who is free of social anxiety can stand up and talk to the media about 'our leaders behaving like children', thereby becoming a role model for climate action by thousands of school pupils all over Europe.

If you look in a different way at the pronounced ways of thinking, seeing and organizing of neurodivergent individuals, it becomes possible to distinguish talents or gifts in addition to the limitations of an atypical brain. This is something that is still talked about far too little. But it is exactly what we are going to do in this book.

## No diagnosis, but on the spectrum

Of course, you don't need to have a diagnosis, like Greta Thunberg, in order to have access to a different, special way of thinking. As mentioned in the introduction, I feel backed up in this by the term 'spectrum', which refers to the fact that traits can be classified and described according to a sliding scale. A spectrum contains every colour of the rainbow and every transition in between.

People with autism are placed on a scale ranging from left – very mild symptoms – to right – very severe symptoms. This is called the 'autistic spectrum', hence the term autism spectrum disorder or ASD. A similar approach is taken in ADHD, but there the scale is referred to as the ADHD continuum. Both conditions have sliding scales from very mild to severe.

Nowadays, people who fall on the right of the spectrum are given a diagnosis. But what if you're looking more towards the left? There you don't have a diagnosis, but you do have certain traits of neurodivergent behaviour, including the strengths and weaknesses. People on the left of the spectrum are often aware of their mild problems, which don't necessarily have a name or label, but unaware of the strengths or even talents associated with them.

As an important side note, there are, of course, other factors that help to determine whether your atypical brain will lead to a successful career. Examples are your environment or level of education. Another key factor is IQ. An IQ below 70 indicates a marked impairment of intellectual capacity. Our argument is not relevant to this particular group, and this book is intended for a different audience: people with average IQs and above. The book is also not for people whose condition affects their quality of life to such an extent that they are unable to function professionally.

Another point to consider is that many mental health conditions are sometimes challenging to differentiate. There are various transitional forms that resemble each other.

A condition doesn't necessarily stay within the box that medicine has devised for it. So it's possible to show traits of different conditions. To express it as a metaphor: just because you have big legs and a trunk doesn't mean you're an elephant. Psychiatrist Menno Oosterhoff writes about this in his book *Ik zie anders niks aan je (You look perfectly normal to me)*: 'A classification sits at symptom level and should not be confused with the condition as a whole.' Classifications of psychological conditions are based on establishing a number of symptoms. After all, a blood sample can't tell you whether someone has ADHD, for example. These classifications are purely a convention; they make it easier for service providers to work with these conditions. But in reality, things are more complex. Oosterhoff therefore argues that we should refer not to a disorder or an abnormality but a picture, a clinical picture that best describes your symptoms. We ourselves have struggled with the right choice of words, but we consciously choose to speak of a difference or an atypical brain. Precisely because we see these differences as something positive. Please note: we don't mean to glorify them. Living with neurodivergence is often anything but easy. And in our experience, daring to name your condition or difference is a crucial first step towards accepting and embracing it.

## The neurodivergent spectrum

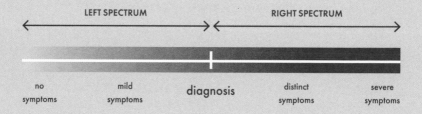

LEFT SPECTRUM            RIGHT SPECTRUM

no
symptoms      mild
symptoms      diagnosis      distinct
symptoms      severe
symptoms

## The left of the spectrum

The left of the spectrum is the side to the left of a diagnosis. Here you have mild symptoms but not enough for an official diagnosis. This part of the spectrum is almost never addressed in books on neurodivergence.

## The right of the spectrum

The right of the spectrum is the side to the right of a diagnosis. Here you have an official diagnosis and distinct symptoms. The further towards the right you are, the more likely the symptoms are to obstruct your normal functioning. It is usually this part of the spectrum that is the focus of research and books on neuro-divergence.

We are often
too shy to admit
our talent,
so let's start
with our
difference

# Chapter 2
# Where are you on the spectrum?

This book takes us on a quest to find your talent, but it begins with a detour. We don't ask what your talent is; we kick off with a different question. We ask what your difference is. Starting from that difference, you can then set out to find what you're good at.

Starting out from your weakness is easier for many people than starting out from what you're good at. Coming from Belgium myself, I can testify that the average Belgian is far too modest to say what they're good at. The answer is usually an acute attack of stammering or the typical 'I can hardly say that about myself, you'd have to ask someone else'. In 2020, HR services company Randstad provided an endearing demonstration of this. In a series of online videos, they asked a number of employees to identify their strengths. It was remarkable to see that nobody could answer. More than that, they all became unsettled, some on the verge of hyperventilating. In the end, they needed the help of their peers to name their strengths. And only when they heard it from an outsider did they accept it – to some extent. Typically Belgian. But perhaps typically human too.

It's high time we become more conscious of our specific talents. Discovering and cultivating them will make it easier to find activities in which we thrive. This might sound logical, but why then do we pay so little attention to it?

For example, the principle that each person has their own unique talents is still not widely endorsed in mainstream education. All too often, the emphasis continues to be on uniform education for all. Even though the principle of a personalized education was understood as long ago as Roman times.

Forgive my occasional digressions into antiquity in this book, but that's all part of my ASD, about which more later. One Roman I would very much like to introduce here is Quintilian. In the first century AD, this renowned orator was already writing about discovering each person's talents and indeed made it his main focus. His ideas can be considered surprisingly current. It's true he was talking about neurotypical students – i.e. people with a 'normal' mental profile – but his claims can just as easily be applied to neurodivergent people.

In Book II of his *Institutes of Oratory*, Quintilian asks whether everyone should be taught according to their unique talent. His answer is visionary. He starts with an apt metaphor: '[...] a gymnastics teacher, when he enters a gymnasium [...] is able to decide for what class of athletic contest each one should be trained'. The same should be done for the mind. Here too, the teacher should be able to detect the talents and abilities of each student and then cultivate them. Quintilian describes it like this: 'Many [...] think it useful to educate students in such a way that their talents are preferably stimulated in the direction they have already taken themselves.'

Quintilian says that your choice of study should be an extension of your talent. To extrapolate, you could argue that your job should also be an extension of that talent. 'One will be better adapted for the study of history, another for poetry, another for law, while some perhaps had better be packed off to the country.' Replace these Roman occupations with, say, those of software programmer, lawyer, lab technician, welder or marketing director, and Quintilian's insights become wonderfully contemporary.

Quintilian goes on to recommend training only in what you are good at. He believes there is no point in correcting things you are bad at. So the Romans knew that too: focus on the positive aspects, don't focus on the negative.

So how do you discover a talent or gift? It's not as simple as it appears at first glance. Only in music or sport is a talent or natural ability immediately apparent. And that's usually because someone else spotted it first. Most of us end up in other sectors, where the talent called for isn't immediately obvious. You may have a knack for languages or mathematics, but 'knack' sounds less flattering than talent, and is also too generic to get you anywhere.

In this book we set out to find your distinct talent, and we do this by starting with your differences. What are you supposedly bad at? What do you always get comments about? What are you ashamed of? We teach you to discover and accept these traits, and help you find the positives they bring or conceal. When an ex-colleague heard I was working on this book, she confessed that she'd been plagued with uncertainty all her life because staff kept saying that, though she was intelligent, she was also 'weird'. Now she knows she has clear symptoms of ASD, she feels encouraged to embrace her 'weirdness' and can see herself as 'special' or even talented.

It is sometimes said that the greatest names in history owe their success to their disorders. Admittedly, this claim should be taken with a pinch of salt, because it's only in recent decades that actual diagnoses have been made. Let's take Albert Einstein as an example, widely recognized as the greatest thinker ever. Of course, he's claimed by just about every organization representing nearly every neuropsychiatric condition. But based on witness accounts, we can say with a degree of certainty that he may have had some form of ASD, specifically the high-functioning autism variant known as Asperger's. Fact is that he did look at the world and the universe with a different logic, a logic that was ground-breaking. We can be more sure about the diagnosis of Virgin Group's Richard Branson, who despite severe dyslexia managed to found a successful student magazine at the age of 16. Even then he had already discovered a talent for motivating others, in this case students who could write well and had a feel for marketing. He came up with the idea, found people to carry it out, better than he could have done himself, and sold it. Becoming a multimillionaire in the process.

So are you actually better off with a condition? As we said earlier, it's not all rosy. Of course, it's often far from easy to be different from the norm. However, in this book, we want to provoke with the statement that abnormally good can be as good or even better than 'normally' good. By the way, what does it mean to be 'normal'? For men, shoe size 42 (UK 8) is considered to be normal. But it's not a case of 'one size fits all'. My hypothesis is that many people deviate from this norm. Not only in their shoe size but also mentally.

Returning to the spectrum and looking at autism, experts talk about a 'spectrum disorder'. This implies that everyone may be somewhere on the spectrum, as we showed in the previous chapter. It's up to you to find out how far along the spectrum you are, and if it can help you to identify your strengths. The same goes for other mental conditions.

ADHD is another condition that comes in degrees. There isn't even an official diagnosis for this condition, which is recognized based on observation and consensus. So in the case of ADHD too, you can say that you may have some of its traits. Perhaps enough to help you identify hidden talents and find out once and for all what kind of work situations you thrive in best, what kind of relationships suit you best and what other benefits you can gain from the condition. The same goes for dyslexia and OCD.

In this book you have to keep asking yourself if you're far enough along the spectrum. If you don't know the answer yourself, ask your family, friends or colleagues. Perhaps they've always known what is different about you. Or look at your children. Some neurodivergent conditions are hereditary: your child may have inherited your eyes or nose, but perhaps also some invisible traits such as the conditions discussed in this book. For me, the epiphany came when my son was officially diagnosed with both ASD and ADHD at the age of six. In my day those tests didn't exist, but his diagnosis suddenly made everything clear to me. Painfully clear at first, but I soon came to see this insight into myself as a gift. It gave me guidance and direction.

To give an idea of the number of diagnoses or labels being handed out nowadays in terms of neuropsychological conditions, we have drawn up the following list. Overall, at least one fifth of the population is estimated to be on the right of the spectrum, which means the figures are even higher than those listed.

Neurodivergence rates in the general population:
→ 5% to 7% of the population is dyslexic (BDA, 2015);
→ 5% of the population is considered to have dyscalculia (BDA, 2015);
→ 5% to 8% of children are diagnosed with ADHD (WHO, 2019);
→ 0.6% to 1.1% of the population is on the autism spectrum. Within this spectrum, just under half have an intellectual impairment; the others are of average to high intelligence (National Autistic Society, 2017 & Zeidan J. et al., 2022);
→ Around 2% have compulsive behaviour or OCD (NVVP, 2023).

## The importance of the right environment

Self-awareness is a first step, but if you're to turn it into self-development, your environment is crucial too. If your employer continues to see you as 'weird', you won't be able to move forward.

Because an understanding environment is vital for people on the spectrum, we devote a separate section of this book to context. If your newfound talent takes you into the right environment, your innate advantage can become even greater. If you meet the right people to team up with, it can make the difference between failure and success. A supreme example of this is Nikola Tesla. I'll come back to him in more detail in Part III, but for now I'll just say that, if not for Elon Musk, his genius might have been forgotten. However, Tesla invented the alternating current generator and patented some three hundred inventions. He even dreamed of being able to photograph thoughts, just to give you some idea of his creativity. An article on the academic news platform *The Conversation* describes him as a 'modern Prometheus', alluding to the Greek hero who stole fire from the gods and was punished for it. This choice of metaphor was not accidental: Nikola Tesla brought lightning to Earth in the form of electricity. He had an amazing eidetic memory and claimed that every idea came to him fully formed in a flash of inspiration. Due to various setbacks and his own rigid attitudes, bizarre habits and odd social behaviour, he never enjoyed the success or fame he deserved. But his main problem was that he didn't always surround himself with the right people.

He needed people who believed in him and would support him unconditionally. Meeting those people heralded a successful period in his life. At other times, having the wrong entourage led to conflict and failure. Tesla is suspected to have had ASD and he certainly had a series of psychotic episodes. Unfortunately, no longlasting collaboration ever materialised between Tesla and his rival Thomas Edison. Both men were brilliant but lacking in empathy. There could only be one vision, their own. Otherwise they might have pioneered even more extraordinary inventions together.

## An appeal for new descriptions

Now that psychiatrists and the school system are beginning to embrace neurodivergence, maybe it's time to rename the classic disorders. ADD would no longer be an attention-deficit disorder but an AFA, an attention focus ability. ADD is indeed the inability to stay focused, but it's also the ability to stay hyper-focused when something genuinely piques your interest. If you find that focus of attention, you don't have an attention deficit. On the contrary, you have an intense ability to focus. The same is true for other conditions. If you have an autism spectrum disorder, you'll find Wally much faster than 'normal' people. If you have ADHD, you may be great at handling a crisis because it's situations like these that give your brain the dopamine hit it always craves.

I wish you great success on this journey of self-discovery. When your strength coincides with something you're passionate about, you are the happiest person on Earth. It might be an existing job in an existing structure. Or it might be a yet-to-be-invented job description in an entirely new work structure. Follow the gift that comes with your difference and find your ideal environment. If you love what you do, you won't live for Fridays, you'll look forward to Mondays.

# Chapter 3
## The physical spectrum

To make the premise of this book – that every difference may conceal a gift – easier to grasp, I'd first like to talk about some physical differences. Here too, there is a spectrum. Applied to physical traits, you can have either a normal or an abnormal physiognomy. That degree of difference can lend a huge advantage, provided that other factors are also present, such as aptitude, perseverance and the right entourage. The analogy with the neuropsychological spectrum is pretty obvious.

### Hands like shovels

Hands like shovels. Pianist's fingers. Built like a tank. Legs like stilts. Elastic limbs. It starts with our use of language, which is full of subtle parallels between physical differences and the benefits they confer.

If size 42 is considered a normal shoe size for men, what can we say about former Australian swimming prodigy Ian Thorpe? Thorpe was the star of the pool at the Sydney 2000 Olympics. Everything about him was remarkable. Barely 17 years old, he was an imposing presence at 6 feet 5 inches tall and had a nickname to strike fear into his rivals' hearts: Thorpedo. A nice play on his family name, but there was more behind it. Thorpe had an exceptionally large shoe size: European size 52. To give some idea of how big that is, you can't order it from on-line retailer Zalando. Most models are available only up to size 49 (UK 13). On one lace-up dress shoe I saw on a website, the listing for size 52 simply read: 'Give us a call'. As if to say, a shoe size of 52 isn't exactly normal. The sheer size of Thorpe's feet enabled him to use them as flippers. I can still see him poised at the finals of the 400 metres freestyle, toes curled over the edge of the starting block. I remember thinking at the time that this was unfair competition: Thorpe should have been competing in the Paralympics. Only Dutch icon Pieter van den Hoogenband ('PVDH' for short) swam faster than the Australian torpedo. But that victory was short-lived, as it spurred Thorpe to train even harder. At the 2001 World Cup in Japan, Thorpe left van den Hoogenband trailing in his wake. As the Dutch press had it: 'PVDH takes on shoe size 52.'

American swimmer Michael Phelps, another Olympic icon, had a physical advantage too. Phelps has Marfan syndrome, a condition that gives him extreme flexibility and unusually long arms and legs. When Phelps spreads out his arms, he is wider than he is tall. That doesn't conform to the ratio of Leonardo da Vinci's perfect man, based on the calculations of Roman architect and writer Vitruvius (another Roman, yes, I know). In his book *De Architectura*, Vitruvius states that 'the length of a man's outstretched arms is equal to his height'. Vitruvius had a whole set of perfect proportions: an ear, he says, is ideally one-third of your head, your feet one-sixth of your body, even the distance from your chin to your nose is fixed with architectural precision. Vitruvius' proportions and da Vinci's drawing based on them are clearly an ode to the norm and not to the outlier.

Height can be another advantage. Let's take the example of two neighbouring countries and great historical rivals: Belgium and the Netherlands. In Belgium, the average man is 180.3 cm tall and the average woman 164.7 cm. The Dutch are slightly taller: their averages are 183.8 cm for men and 170.7 cm for women. You could say the Dutch have an advantage over the Belgians: the Dutch have an average head start of around 3 cm in every sport. In some sports this doesn't matter all that much but, in others, it does. The Netherlands traditionally wins many more medals than Belgium at the Olympics, although of course this is partly down to mindset and environment.

It's not just height that can be an advantage: any difference in terms of limbs, organs or senses can work in your favour. Being bigger, having longer limbs, having larger organs than average. All of these differences carry an advantage within certain contexts. Take cyclist Egan Bernal, for example, who won the Tour de France in 2019 and the Giro d'Italia in 2021. Bernal has a very high $VO_2$ max, a measure of the amount of oxygen the body can use during exercise. Bernal's figures are considered 'exceptional', for which read excessive, disproportionate.

I find it strange that Paralympic athletes – i.e. athletes with an impairment – who want to compete need to hold a classification stating their impairment and the class they are to compete in. This isn't the case for 'normal' athletes, except in sports like boxing or judo, where competitors are classed by weight. Everyone thinks it entirely logical that a super flyweight (under 52kg) shouldn't be put up against a heavyweight in the ring. But a swimmer of Thorpe's proportions is able to compete against an opponent of statistically average height and average shoe size.

In short, physical differences can be plotted on a spectrum just like mental differences. And here too, there is a left and right side of the spectrum. If you are lucky enough to fall on the left side of the spectrum, you can fairly easily use it to your advantage as an athlete. The analogy with mental abnormalities is striking. Awareness of your abnormality and the associated talent can – metaphorically speaking – help you jump further. But even if you fall on the right of the spectrum, you may still have an opportunity to turn your difference into your talent.

# We have two ears but only one mouth, perhaps we could listen a bit more

Liesbeth Dillen, business coach, keynote speaker and co-founder of YIN United

# Chapter 4
## Special compensations

A physical difference or disability can also confer a professional advantage beyond the world of elite sport. A good example is business coach Liesbeth Dillen, who founded the coaching firm YIN United with this book's co-author, Emily Rammant. Liesbeth is now a respected business coach, but at one point she was actually set to become CEO of IKEA Belgium and Netherlands. Just as she was about to take that step, a benign tumour was diagnosed on her thyroid. Not a problem in itself, but a medical error during surgery left her with 70% paralysis of her vocal cords. She couldn't take in enough breath and effectively lost her voice. With intense therapy, she managed to reduce her impairment to 30%, but the fact remained that she could no longer use her voice properly. Unfortunately, your voice is a pretty essential tool if you're a CEO wanting to steer meetings and communicate with your many IKEA colleagues.

Fortunately, something odd but amazing happened in Liesbeth's life. As a result of her impairment, she started to talk less, but also began to listen better and better. And listening just happens to be the perfect skill for a coach. Liesbeth often says that we humans would do better to reflect on the fact that we've been given two ears, two eyes and only one mouth. Reading body language and analyzing voice pitch provides a wealth of additional information about how someone is feeling, which is key information in a coaching session. Liesbeth now also had more time to take a helicopter view and spot potential in the commercial, strategic or operational challenges facing her clients. And to explore the career opportunities still open to her after the harsh sentence of a life-long disability. A limitation she wasn't prepared to give in to, and did her utmost to escape. But now it turns out she can't escape it, at least she's reaping its benefits, more specifically the ability to listen more effectively and handle silence.

In the music world, there are countless examples. Ray Charles became completely blind at age seven due to the eye disease glaucoma, but still went on to become a pioneer of soul music in the 1950s, winning seventeen Grammy Awards, five of them posthumously. Neurologists now talk about the Ray Charles effect when someone's hearing improves as a result of blindness. Neurologists in the US have effectively discovered that nerve cells work together so that the different senses support each other, and the loss of one sense strengthens the functioning of another. A physical difference that at first glance is a disadvantage can still turn into an advantage.

A physical limitation can boost a scientific career too. The most dramatic example is that of Stephen Hawking, the theoretical physicist, astrophysicist, cosmologist and eminent scientist whose ALS diagnosis at age 21 spurred him to develop extreme perseverance and devote his entire career to understanding the universe, leading to ground-breaking work on relativity theory and black holes. Despite his severe limitations and extensive care needs, Hawking has received dozens of international awards for his scientific research. Doctors had initially given him only two years to live. Talk about perseverance.

Of course, we can't expect everyone to become a Stephen Hawking or a Ray Charles. These are exceptional examples of people with physical limitations, and I certainly wouldn't claim that every person with a physical difference has the capacity to become famous. But this does lead us to the central idea of this book, to be explored more in the next chapter, namely that difference can bring an advantage. And that becoming aware of this advantage can lead to a successful life.

**Liesbeth Dillen, business coach, keynote speaker and co-founder of YIN United**
*30% vocal cord paralysis*

———

'I'm 100% back to work. The result of not giving up and a zest for life. And of love. Love for life, for my daughter. I had a choice. Do I fight against something, or for something? What to do with my 30% air? Do I fight the hospital with a legal case? This wasn't America, of course. It wasn't a screenplay where I'd "win through in the end", physically broken but rich. I was facing a predicted fight of easily ten years against a behemothic university hospital and its army of lawyers. Wouldn't it be better to fight to stretch the limits of my recovery as far as possible and regain more of my air and voice?

I chose the latter. Fighting to live more again. And to give. My motto is that you don't choose everything that happens to you in life, but you do always have the freedom and power to choose how to deal with it. I didn't put that 30% into negative energy, I wanted to be a mum who could build a den in the woods with her daughter again, go on cycling holidays, sing and dance. That was my drive. I travelled all over the country to find doctors to help me. I tried everything, from electroshock treatment to relearning to speak, to breathe. Greedy as I was to get better. And it worked.

My voice has changed, I have changed, my job has changed completely, my whole life has changed. My voice is now nicer, richer, warmer and deeper. At least if I let it come from my belly and soul. Then something warm emerges. Before stepping onto a stage, I consciously try to bring my soul into my voice so I'm not just a talking head. The effect is that I'm more human and accessible, and probably come across as more vulnerable and transparent. I don't have to pretend to be Mrs Perfect who knows everything. That creates distance and I don't want that. If I just dare to be myself, I can connect with the audience. And I can hear that by the way my voice sounds. A different sound, depth, vibe. In the end, as a person, you're remembered mainly for how you made people feel, not for what you said.'

# What stands in the way
# becomes the way

Marcus Aurelius, Roman emperor and Stoic philosopher

# PART II

# The mental spectrum

Evolution is made possible by flaws in the mainstream. Those flaws are people with a difference

# Chapter 5
# A plea for
# neurodiversity

Neurodiversity refers to variation or diversity in human cognitive function: the way the brain works. Every brain is unique – as unique as a fingerprint – and we all have different skills, needs and abilities. Neurodivergence refers to types of cognitive function that are not considered 'typical' and deviate from the norm. This often means that neurodivergent people themselves are seen as 'deviating' or different. Which is strange, because in recent decades and indeed centuries quite a few scholars have unwittingly developed techniques for thinking like people with neurodivergent abilities.

Take the well-known 'lateral thinking' technique devised by psychologist Edward de Bono in the 1970s. Lateral thinking starts from the assumption that a problem has a beginning and an end, and that a 'normal' person tends to take the shortest route between the two. Used as an exercise, it solves a problem by taking surprising detours. Which happens to be exactly how someone with ADHD operates. They don't go straight from A to B, but wander through the alphabet, coming up with surprising, innovative and unforeseen solutions along the way.

Upon closer examination, it can be observed that numerous creative thinking techniques are essentially imitations of the thinking processes of a neurodivergent mind. And they're nothing new: they don't date from this century or even last century. You guessed it: the Romans already had thinking techniques for looking at the world differently. The Stoics believed that we can't choose what happens to us, but we *can* choose how we react to it. If we can't do anything about a situation, we'd do better to resign ourselves to it. The term 'stoic' in this sense has entered the dictionary to describe a school of philosophy that specializes in enduring things. But Stoic thinking isn't like that at all. They simply resign themselves to things they can't change. For example, there's no point in getting irrationally worked up over receiving a speeding ticket, because you can't change that. Far more interesting is the Stoic view that every event is an invitation to see things differently, to take advantage, to learn. Their motto is 'prosperity through adversity'. Therefore, instead of responding to a situation with a negative 'Oh no', a Stoic approaches it with a positive 'Yes, but.' They see the ability to reframe setbacks as an important skill. In his *Meditations*, Roman emperor Marcus Aurelius describes it as follows: 'What stands in the way becomes the way.' Liesbeth Dillen draws her resilience from this too, as you saw earlier. It might seem counter-intuitive to a 'normal' thinker, but it's a totally natural way of thinking for a neurodivergent person.

Stoics see setbacks as a learning process, teaching us to accept and rethink situations, arriving at a different perspective on the world. Until now, this different perspective has been appreciated and cultivated only among philosophers, psychologists, inventors and other creative thinkers. But it's time to appreciate this thinking style in people who think inherently differently and by their nature come up with surprising solutions. American psychologist Devon MacEachron agrees. In a 2018 interview, she argues it is time to stop marginalising neurodivergence as an abnormality and instead see it as an enrichment. She goes so far as to say that neurodiversity is part of our genes and ensures the evolution of humanity. The genes for autism and ADHD are not errors, but a variation in the human genome that ensures progress.

In the following chapters I come to the heart of the matter: first I describe a neurological disorder to get readers started on recognizing the symptoms, plotting themselves within the spectrum and discovering the potential accompanying gifts. From there, I bridge the gap to a work setting. This pattern is repeated for four neuropsychological disorders: AD(H)D (attention-deficit (hyperactivity) disorder), ASD (autism spectrum disorder), dyslexia and OCD (obsessive-compulsive disorder).

You're not
from another
planet,
your talents
are

# Chapter 6
# Autism spectrum disorder (ASD)

## All hail the specialist!

We live in a society that is committed to specialisms. This is most evident in our education system, which quickly steers you in one direction and places the emphasis on excelling in a single domain. Fortunately, such a society is fertile ground for people with autism spectrum disorder. People with this diagnosis will never be good at everything, but they can definitely excel at certain things. It's usually the life goal of parents and teachers to find this gift.

But please note: this is not an argument for enforced specialization. A reverse trend is underway in society, a trend that is swinging the pendulum back to generalists, and I can only welcome it. Specialization has its limits, and indeed has significant drawbacks, described very convincingly in two significant books from 2019 and 2018, namely *Range: How Generalists Triumph in a Specialized World* by David Epstein and *The Polymath: Unlocking the Power of Human Versatility* by Waqas

Ahmed. Both authors make a case for the homo universalis, with Leonardo da Vinci as its prototype. It's claimed you would need thirteen specialists from as many different fields to make one Leonardo da Vinci. Both Epstein and Ahmed believe that the world belongs to universalists. They alone have an array of interests that enables them to respond flexibly to the rapidly changing world around us. Both authors therefore advocate a broad set of interests and a generalist approach.

But I believe there is still a crucial need for specialists, although they obviously need to find and inspire each other. Perhaps that cross-fertilization will be driven by generalists, getting all of the different experts working seamlessly together.

Either way, it's good news for people with ASD, as they can continue to contribute based on their unique gifts and develop into specialists. Individuals with a single distinct talent have the potential to truly change our world through their insights. In my view, this also applies to people who are a bit further towards the left on the spectrum (and so don't have a diagnosis but recognize its traits in themselves).

Famous people with possible autistic traits include Franz Kafka, Henry Ford, Steve Jobs, Vincent van Gogh, American chess prodigy Bobby Fischer, Abraham Lincoln and Bill Gates, to name but a few. On a crucial qualifying note, some of these 'diagnoses' are retrospective and based on witness accounts, as the term 'autism' was not coined until 1943. But we can wonder what our world would be like had people with ASD traits not been able to display their special talent.

# What is ASD?

Autism spectrum disorder (ASD) was researched and identified by Leo Kanner in 1943 and Hans Asperger in 1944, working independently of each other. Kanner, a children's psychiatrist associated with the University of Baltimore, described characteristic symptoms in eleven children, including lack of interest in social contact, a strong need for routines and various learning difficulties. Conversely, some of these children also had a highly developed memory or verbal talent. Austrian paediatrician Hans Asperger arrived at more or less the same findings. Until recently, the term 'Asperger' was applied to children with a mild to severe form of ASD coupled with high intelligence. Asperger himself talked about 'little professors', because the children in his study could expound on their favourite subjects with astonishing depth of knowledge and attention to detail. Nowadays, the term 'Asperger syndrome' is no longer used in official circles and we refer only to 'autism spectrum disorder'.

ASD, as the name suggests, encompasses a *spectrum*. This means that each individual is situated at a unique point on the spectrum, indicating that there are varying degrees of autism and no two people are located at exactly the same point. Or, as Dr Stephen Shore puts it: 'If you know one person with autism, you know one person with autism.' The best-known traits of ASD are the negative ones. People with ASD have problems with social contact. They can seem hesitant, they may have trouble maintaining a conversation, or find it hard to empathize with someone else's feelings. This might cause them to make honest but blunt comments that come across as inappropriate. And they often have difficulties with figurative language because they take everything literally.

Our son Noah was diagnosed with ASD at the age of six. There was a time when he was very anxious; he felt as if he was constantly being followed. It started early in the morning at the breakfast table, where he kept anxiously peering over his shoulder to check there was no one standing there. At our repeated urging, Noah finally dared to admit why he was so scared: 'In class they said Jesus is always behind you.' We had to pull out all the proverbial stops to explain that he shouldn't take this literally, but it was clear that when talking to Noah you should avoid expressions such as 'break a leg', 'it's raining cats and dogs' or 'he's a wolf in sheep's clothing'.

Other autistic traits are a strong need for routine and marked repetitive behaviour. People with ASD can perform the same movement over and over without ever tiring of it. It is assumed that an autistic brain processes information in a slightly different way. The brain filters too little, too much, or the wrong information. This explains why people with ASD often have difficulty processing sensory information. It can also affect their body perception and coordination, giving them a stiff and awkward appearance.

So much for the negative picture. There are also many traits that could be described as talents. For example, people with ASD may have an exceptional feeling for language, an extreme eye for detail, highly developed visual and spatial recognition, an excellent memory or a talent for organizing and ordering the world around them. They also recognize patterns more quickly. We all know the expression: once is an accident, twice a coincidence, three times a pattern. I sometimes recognize patterns after only one occurrence, even at the risk of being perceived as 'quick to judge'. However, those who know me better understand that a single instance could be a coincidence or the indication of a pattern. While I do not claim to be infallible, when I have been correct our company has been able to respond more swiftly than our competitors. Dr Annelies Spek, an authority on autism in adults, has long insisted on the importance of highlighting the strengths of those with autism: 'Being more attentive to the talents of people with autism can help to raise their self-esteem. Practising something you're good at can also contribute to a sense of purpose, because it means you're also of value to society.'

All too often, the diagnosis fails to focus enough on what is going well, what the talents are. Yet it is precisely this information that is vital to integrate into your future path in life. By the way, according to the authors of *Savant skills in autism: psychometric approaches and parental reports,* special talents occur in 28.5% to 62.5% of people with autism.

## Where are you on the spectrum?

The diagnosis of ASD is made by a multidisciplinary team. But – once again – it's all about a spectrum. People with a diagnosis are on the right of the spectrum. Perhaps you're more towards the left. In this case you might be flying 'under the radar' of a diagnosis but clearly recognize some traits of ASD in yourself. For example, if you have difficulty with social contact and need lots of structure, if you don't like unexpected visitors or a change of plans, you probably have some form of ASD. It's true, however, that an actual diagnosis will only follow if you score high enough on every aspect.

Why not try asking those around you. Your parents, partner, friends or colleagues are bound to have anecdotes to share about your unusual behaviour. I experienced this myself in 2021 when I 'outed' my own neuropsychological differences. My first art director, who I formed a creative team with back in 1995, replied: 'I knew that before you did.' It is highly probable that those around you figured it out long before you did yourself.

If you recognize one or more ASD traits in yourself, congratulations! These traits can point the way towards naming your gift.

Do you recognize any of the following strengths in yourself?

- ☐ You have extreme attention to detail. You spot things that no one else would notice.
- ☐ You see structure, you see systems.
- ☐ You want clear rules and expectations, and any departures from them make you uncomfortable.
- ☐ You have special interests that can keep you engaged for hours.
- ☐ Your senses are easily overstimulated by the world around you. Sound in particular can be overwhelming. This hypersensitivity can also confer an advantage, such as excellent hearing.
- ☐ You have a tendency to daydream.
- ☐ You are solution-focused and find solutions faster than most people around you.
- ☐ You are good with words and have an extensive vocabulary.
- ☐ Your memory is more accurate than Google Search and also goes back further in time.
- ☐ You are visually oriented and have good spatial awareness.
- ☐ You are a stickler for justice and honesty.
- ☐ You are very honest in dealings with other people, sometimes too honest.

Let's remind ourselves of the central message of this book: focus not on what you can't do, but on what you can. For example, as parents we're already trying to figure out where our son's aptitudes lie. In early 2020, we took Noah to a Keith Haring retrospective at BOZAR, the Centre for Fine Arts in Brussels. We could see right away that he was fascinated by the drawings of interlocking figures and objects that filled the walls. Maybe they felt to him like systems. When we collected the tickets, Noah picked up an exhibition brochure of his own accord. He unfolded the whole thing like an old map, glanced at the dozens of photos of the artworks on display, then folded the brochure back up again. In the first exhibition room, Noah enthusiastically pointed to a work: 'That painting is here.' He opened the brochure and, without looking, promptly pointed to the right work. Throughout the visit, he kept doing this for each and every artwork in the brochure, as if he'd compiled it himself. He found this game highly amusing; we could barely keep up as he sped through the exhibition rooms and scarcely had time to enjoy the exhibits ourselves. But we didn't mind all that much; we could always come back another day if need be. We felt it was more important to follow our son's pace. As we neared the end of the exhibits, he spun round and intoned in a serious voice: 'This is the only one we haven't seen yet.' I was worried for a moment that we'd have to redo all the rooms, because he's capable of that, but he seemed happy with the outcome.

We record these sorts of events in a notebook, in the hope that a clear thread will emerge after a few years. What's already clear is that Noah has strong visual recognition. He also has a feel for creating systems and a vivid imagination. The question remains, of course, to which direction or skill set we can link this in a later professional setting. Fortunately, we still have time to decide that.

# WANTED: WOMAN WITH AUTISM

Autism was once believed to be primarily a condition affecting males, as early studies conducted in the 1940s focused on males as the target group. This skewed perception of autism prevalence has since been disproven, with a recognition that autism is just as common in women as it is in men. However, the manifestation of autism in women is often different due to the development of unique coping mechanisms, making diagnosis more challenging. For instance, autistic women may only be diagnosed after experiencing an emotional crisis, as they tend to internalize and conceal the challenges associated with their condition through camouflaging or 'masking' (Solomon et al., 2012). Traditionally, girls are often required to take part in social interactions from a young age, while it is more acceptable for boys to go off and play. As a result of these masking techniques, autism is still largely considered a male-centric condition, leading to a 'male bias' in diagnostic methods and clinical expectations.

## In what work environment do you thrive best?

One work environment is not like another. Though I've never had an ASD diagnosis, it was immediately clear to me what kind of work environment just didn't suit me. No open-plan offices for me, no rooms with too many auditory stimuli and no jobs requiring constant social interaction. In my first job as an editor at a local weekly magazine, all of the staff had to wear the same grey suit, with a pale blue shirt and a tie. I do have my routines, but I prefer to decide them myself. When routines are imposed, I instinctively try to evade or sabotage them. In the few years I worked at that magazine, I never wore the whole uniform. I always pushed the boundaries, pairing the suit jacket with jeans, or the grey trousers with a casual pullover. A few years later, when I moved to Brussels and started work as a junior copywriter, my favourite thing was to go and sit in one of the corner offices. This attracted the odd smattering of comments, but I didn't see a corner office as a career goal. For me, it was mainly a quiet place where I was free of all the stimuli of an open-plan office.

Know that autistic traits are not limited to sensitivity to sound, but can also manifest in sensitivity to bright light or being allergic to a lot of movement. This affects the level of concentration at work. Some individuals also need extra time to switch from one task to another without warning. An entirely different aspect of sensory sensitivity is sensitivity to taste and smell. People with autism experience everything they see under a magnifying glass, everything they hear through a stethoscope, and everything they feel through sensitively tuned sensors.

By the way, if you want, you can have your own sensory profile or stimulus profile drawn up by a professional such as an occupational therapist or autism coach. A typical characteristic of ASD is that you can be oversensitive to certain things and under-sensitive to others. A sudden sound is not something that someone with ASD just hears; it assaults all the senses in a very intrusive way. Recently, when I was out running, a passer-by's dog suddenly barked. This hit me so hard that I felt a strain coming on in my hamstrings. In that sense, sound can be an attack on my entire system. There will always be unexpected sounds, such as an engine firing somewhere, but in the meantime, I try to avoid loud noises as much as possible. So you won't see me at a festival very often. The few times I do go, I mainly seek out remote stages where the music is quieter. Ukrainian autism specialist Olga Bogdashina has compiled a series of questions on this topic in a *Sensory Profile Checklist*, which now forms the basis for sensory research in people with ASD. This allows care providers to offer targeted sensory support.

If you have autism, it's also a good idea to think about how predictable or unpredictable a job is. Belgian online marketer Elise Cordaro studied journalism out of an intrinsic interest in the subject, but struggled with the practical side of the job. Think about establishing contacts, making phone calls, the lack of fixed hours, waiting around for something newsworthy to happen, and so on. She might have chosen a different degree course if she'd known this beforehand (her diagnosis came after her degree).

By the way, Elise explains very clearly on her blog why speaking on the phone is so difficult for someone with ASD: 'I'm very visually oriented and rely heavily on body language in communicating with others. It helps me understand people better and figure out what they are thinking, but I also use it myself to get my message across. For example, I use a lot of hand gestures. And smiling or nodding for a while is helpful when you can't immediately find the right words and need time to think. When making a phone call, nonverbal cues such as body language are not available. This means I'm less able to understand what the person on the other end is saying and I also find it harder to express myself. So a phone conversation takes much more effort and is more prone to misunderstandings. People also tend to feel more uncomfortable with silences and may rush to fill them, resulting in faster communication compared to a face-to-face meeting. Using the phone is a source of stress, confusion and exhaustion for me. I try to avoid it as much as possible. But when I do have to make a call, it always entails a huge amount of preparation. I prepare the conversation topic by listing what I need to say and thinking up answers to possible questions. This gives me a sort of flow chart with different scenarios. I also set out a notebook and pen to take notes, a glass of water for my dry throat (due to nerves) and try to limit ambient noise by closing windows and turning off notifications.'

If you have traits of ASD, you may find more job satisfaction in a job where social interaction is less important or irrelevant. Software company Ultranauts, headquartered in New York, 'gets' this completely. This venture by former MIT engineers Art

Shectman and Rajesh Anandan aims not only to build a successful company, but also to show that neurodivergence can give a distinct edge in business. The Ultranauts website claims that 75% of their staff have ASD and boasts of a 50% annual growth rate. The company achieves that only by excelling in their field, which they do by fully utilizing the talent of their engineers with ASD. However, the co-founders do stress that profit is not the company's sole raison d'être. They want to show that people with ASD deserve a chance and can even make your business better. 'We're going up against global IT firms and performing significantly better,' said Ultranauts CEO Rajesh Anandan in an interview with *Fast Company* business magazine. 'We're staffing these teams with fantastically capable talent who just haven't had a fair shot before.' The company shows respect and understanding for each individual. For example, you're not expected to make social contact. If you want, you can communicate with your colleagues solely via Slack, a messaging app for teams.

A work environment that respects your talent and understands your need for isolation is of paramount importance if you have autism. It's this need for isolation in particular that can make things hard in practice for people with autism. Office politics can be a mystery to some people with ASD, whose honesty and sense of justice mean they are uninterested in gossip or elbowing their way to the top. Possibly missing out on promotion. That ASD can add value in the workplace is also confirmed by Belgian companies TRplus and Passwerk, which also focus on getting professionals with autism hired in mainstream employment. To date they have identified four areas of expertise, with more to come. For example, they offer software testers and developers who excel in high-quality software thanks to their logical thinking skills. Because people with autism are often unparalleled in following rules and procedures, their code is extremely pure. And they generally have a highly developed creativity that enables them to come up with innovative solutions in various programming languages. Other job categories include business intelligence consultants, who help companies to process big data, and X-ray screening staff, who use their highly developed visual thinking skills to screen airport baggage. 'We are known for being excellent at focusing,' said one employee with autism. 'That's why we can keep this work up for eight hours at a stretch. Our other colleagues – and I do believe I can say this – wouldn't be able to do that. I think our focus is our greatest asset.' That this focus can save lives is something the Israeli military has known for some time. It has a special unit, Unit 9900, for autistic people with attention to detail. Their job is to detect suspicious objects or movements in satellite images.

# What jobs can you excel in?

The right work environment is one key aspect, but what job content will make you happy? For most people, this is a never-ending quest, starting as early as their choice of studies. Being on the spectrum might make it easy for you to find your talent. It will be a gift that allows you to excel in one domain, and with a little luck maybe in two domains. As people with ASD traits often love systems, I've come up with a simple formula to help you find your passion:

Unique interest + Special gift + Adapted work environment
= PROFESSIONAL SUCCESS

## Interests

People with ASD have clear fields of interest to which they can devote themselves with a one-track mind. Those interests may seem unorthodox but having one gives you a head start on people who are not on the spectrum and are a little bit interested in most things.

Do you have a special focus on a single subject that you can explore endlessly? See it as a gift. By now you know I have a thing for the Roman Empire, and more specifically the Byzantine Empire. Don't ask me why, I just do. I'm not sure this passion takes me anywhere in life. 'Enough is enough,' said my wife. Inspired by the Netflix series *Atypical,* she gives me up to three cards a day I can use if I want to mention the Romans. But I do believe it's better to be truly interested in something rather than just find everything a bit 'meh'. A colleague recently expressed frustration with his 12-year-old daughter. She'd been asked at school what her passions were and, despite having good marks all round, she couldn't get beyond 'gymnastics'. With further prompting, she listed a few more subjects, but without much conviction. My colleague can already see it coming: later on she'll have the intellect for further study, but won't know what to choose. Things are different when you feel the influence of the spectrum. For example, as a child with a tendency towards compulsive behaviour, you'll build a collection of rocks, or want to know all there is to know about dinosaurs, or transform Transformers until you can take one apart and put it back together by yourself, or learn the names of every Roman emperor by heart starting with the first official emperor Augustus, or need to know how special effects are created in sci-fi, or something else. One interest might be more useful than another, but often it can still put a child on the path to the right choice of studies and later the right profession. Because that Transformer enthusiast might grow up to become a good electrician or engineer. That budding dinosaur expert might be able to indulge their interest in a more academic direction. And so on.

Sometimes you don't know it yourself if your interests are overpowering. But rest assured, to your parents or friends those interests stand out just as clearly as a shiny coin in a fountain. A true lucky charm. Ask them about your interests and your behaviour; you'll notice that they don't see you in the same way you see yourself. They can show you the path to happiness.

What is your coin in the fountain? What can you go on about endlessly? If your coin isn't quite clear yet, keep a notebook and jot down the things that preoccupy you and why. After several months a pattern will emerge. This is your path.

## Special gift

Once you've found your interest, you need to link it to your special gift. People on the spectrum (with a high enough IQ) possess one or more of the talents described below.

## Exceptional memory

Do you remember details that others forget? Do you find it easy to retain a lot of information? Or can you retrieve memories and recount them with absurd attention to detail? If so, you're somewhere on the spectrum among people with exceptional memory. Combining that memory with an interest can lead to interesting results. As a teenager, I once memorized the names and reigns of all the Roman emperors. Not for a test, just out of interest. As I dredged that memory up for this book, I suddenly recalled that 69 AD was a three-emperor year, with Otho, Galba and Vitellius. My friends back then found it pretty bizarre that I would memorize such things. To make it seem a little less weird, I wrote a rap about the Roman Empire in the style of the very first rappers Grandmaster Flash and The Furious Five. I don't know if that helped me come across as less weird to my friends, maybe not. But now I look back on it, an academic career as a historian might have been another field I'd have felt right at home in, with my gift for remembering things + interest in the Roman Empire + need for a quiet working environment.

Depending on your interests and memory skills, these could be jobs for you:
→ Academic
→ Sports journalist
→ Historian
→ Musician
→ Researcher
→ Biologist
→ Judicial expert
→ Librarian
→ Legal officer
→ Financial trader
→ Computer expert
→ Systems analyst

Note that none of this is black-and-white. A researcher nowadays doesn't sit on their own in a lab all the time, but often has to work in a team. Not all financial traders are alike: if your job mostly involves focusing on figures (nice and impersonal, no people to deal with), that's fine. If customer contact is part of your role, the job might not be ideal for you. And so on.

## Attention to detail

Studies have shown that people with ASD have an extra-sharp attention to detail. Their eagle eye allows them to spot anomalies, changes, patterns, etc. with striking ease. Here is a small selection of jobs that really need extreme attention to detail:

→ Lab technician
→ Radiologist
→ Antiquarian
→ Restorer
→ Visual artist or word artist
→ Biologist
→ Designer
→ Chocolatier
→ Archaeologist
→ Scientific illustrator
→ Computer programmer
→ Airport X-ray screener
→ Intelligence officer

## Systemizer

Systems thinkers see patterns everywhere. Do you have a natural talent for recognizing, analyzing and/or assembling systems? Then that makes you a systems thinker too. If you're quite far towards the right on the spectrum, it may even feel like there's a pattern to everything. That promptly opens up a whole range of jobs in which you can excel:
→ Software architect
→ Computer programmer
→ Statistical researcher
→ Private investigator
→ Consultant
→ Data analyst
→ Financial planner


## Verbal strengths

Some people with ASD compensate for their lack of emotional intelligence or 'EQ' with a higher verbal IQ. Language is their playground: not for making social contact, but for exploration. These verbal strengths are usually combined with an ability to remember vast amounts of trivia. Jobs that require verbal strengths include:
→ Writer
→ Columnist
→ Screenwriter

→ Podcast maker
→ Public speaker
→ Stand-up comedian
→ Reporter
→ Editor
→ Teacher

## To sum up

We've seen that people with ASD require an adapted work environment, often have a unique interest and may also have special talents. Earlier I mentioned the Netflix series *Atypical*, in which an 18-year-old boy with ASD finds his field of study by combining his passion for the Antarctic, attention to detail and talent for drawing as a future scientific illustrator. A real-life current example is American professor Temple Grandin. Her special gift is visual thinking, her specific interest is animal welfare and, in becoming a zoologist, she chose a work environment that was right for her. Her three paths converged in a mission to make livestock farms and slaughterhouses more animal-friendly by designing facilities that respect the animals' natural behaviour and so make them calmer, leading to higher-quality, less expensive meat. Grandin's visual talent enabled her to imagine perfectly what those facilities should look like. She also designed and built herself a 'hug machine'. Modelled on a device used for cattle, it was intended to soothe her ASD anxiety by compressing her body between two boards.

Grandin's achievements confirm the formula given at the start of this chapter:

Unique interest + Special gift + Adapted work environment = PROFESSIONAL SUCCESS

**Elise Cordaro, online marketer and author**
*ASD and ADHD*

---

Neurological conditions are not always easy to tell apart, as Elise confirms with her dual diagnosis.

'I was actually diagnosed quite late, though I'd felt different for some time. The psychologists I saw during my studies were all of the opinion that there was "nothing wrong with me", even though I was struggling with serious concentration and sleep problems. I also felt very lonely in my teens; it was hard to connect with others. In the end I was only diagnosed with ADHD at 26, and autism at 27. I actually discovered both diagnoses myself, and then had them confirmed by professionals. How did I discover them? Simply by hearing some classmates talking about ADD. It seemed like a possible cause of my concentration problems. Only I didn't quite fit the picture of ADHD, as I'm very systematic and not at all impulsive, and I didn't recognize myself in the social aspect. Then I wondered if autism might be involved too. My boyfriend at the time had autism and when I read a book about the symptoms it seemed to have been written specifically about me. The ASD diagnosis that followed didn't come to me as bad news, but a relief. Even the team of experts was amazed at how well I'd managed to hide my autism.

I've known for some time that there are also positive sides to my "being different", such as my zeal and creativity. Give me an hour and I can develop a new hobby. Another positive trait is my problem-solving ability. When I have a problem and start talking about it, I'm already solving it in my head. I can picture things easily and see patterns everywhere. I can often predict how something will turn out and where it might go wrong. And I have an eye for detail. At work, I'll never let a double space in a text pass unnoticed. I'm also very sensitive to colour nuances. God is in the details, the details make the whole.

For me, it was important to have my diagnoses in black and white so I was no longer seen as exaggerating. It's like being descended from an ancient tribe of people, thinking you're the last remaining survivor, then suddenly being told that they've found your family. Since that day, I no longer feel alone. I never feel down anymore and am at ease in my own skin.

I used to miss connection with other people, but now I realize I was mainly missing a connection with myself. Since getting to know myself better, I've become more open to other people. Now I can talk openly about autism and ADHD, and I can be more honest. Because I'm more authentic, I now connect with others more easily. My advice would be, most importantly get to know yourself and don't pay too much heed to other people's advice. The journey can be fun, it doesn't have to be all bad. If you have a brain that works differently and want to find ways to function well, you'll have to let go of convention and, above all, find your own path.'

# For a brainstorming session all you need is yourself

# Chapter 7
## Attention Deficit Hyperactivity Disorder (ADHD)

## What is ADHD/ADD?

Where autism talks about a spectrum, ADHD and ADD talk about a continuum, which comes down to the same thing. So maybe you're not far enough along the continuum to officially have ADHD as well, but your traits are prominent enough for you to discover your own strengths.

Did anyone ever say of you: 'They just can't sit still'? If so, maybe you're already somewhere on the continuum. I have some ADHD traits myself. If I have to queue somewhere for more than ten minutes, I start pacing. If a meeting lasts for over half an hour, I'll stand up to signal it's time to wrap up. My mind wanders easily when I'm bored, prompting colleagues to say: 'I think we've lost Peter.'

And I've never had a fixed spot for my desk. I've always made a statement of this, because I work nomadically and enjoy having unscheduled meetings with everyone. But it's also inspired by the fact I feel trapped when I 'have to' sit somewhere; I want to be free.

My symptoms are clear to my colleagues, but they're mild compared to those of my colleague Jef, who's quite a bit further to the right on the continuum. One lunchtime during a period of Zen-like calm in our open-plan office, he came rushing in with a cup of coffee, making an excessive amount of noise. He flung open his laptop, almost knocking his coffee over in the process. His behaviour was the exact opposite of everyone else's, as they sat there quietly working away. For the benefit of everyone in the office, whether interested or not, Jef announced the reason for his behaviour: 'Sorry, guys, but this morning was so busy I still need to adjust to the fact that it's so quiet now.' An ADHD brain has difficulty handling quiet times. It always needs sufficient stimuli. There always has to be one or more conflicts or tasks constantly on the boil.

A person with ADHD has difficulty sitting still, both physically and mentally, as their thoughts continuously jump from one topic to another. So ADHD or ADD (I'll come back later to the difference between the two) is not a gift in a society where you have to wait your turn at the baker's or to contribute in a discussion and where most jobs see you assigned to a fixed desk. But ADHD *is* a gift when you find the right working conditions, the right work content and the right theme. Jef has managed to do this. He is an account director at a communications agency where he manages communications for several brands. He can switch between car brands, beer brands and other brands, he shuttles physically between agency and client and every briefing is a challenge that demands a solution by a given deadline. The perfect job for someone with ADHD. Put Jef somewhere he has to do the same thing every day, for the same client, in the same place, and it will make him deeply unhappy.

## The symptoms: daydreamers and blabbermouths

AD(H)D is a neurobiological developmental disorder that causes attention problems, disorganization and hyperreactivity/impulsivity. While a lot of research has been done on ADHD and ADD in recent decades, there is no medical or psychological test that incontrovertibly 'proves' ADHD. The diagnosis is made by a doctor in consultation with other healthcare professionals, and only after extensive interviews, lengthy observation and neuropsychological testing.

In the past, a distinction was often drawn between ADD and ADHD, with the 'H' standing for 'hyperactivity'. Nowadays only 'ADHD' is used, irrespective of whether the person is also hyperactive. In simple terms, you could say that those with ADHD are the blabbermouths whereas those with ADD are the daydreamers. Indeed, the latter are often remarkably silent and passive. As with ASD, the diagnosis is sometimes missed in girls because they are less often perceived as hyperactive, tending to be seen instead as disorganized or chaotic.

The reason why ADHD is not recognized so easily in girls is probably because they lack the 'H'.

But there is more to ADHD than being a blabbermouth or having a wandering mind. Three traits determine whether you have ADHD and which form of it you have:

1. Attention problems
2. Hyperactivity
3. Impulsivity

Concentration problems are typical of all forms of ADHD. This trait is not always appreciated by others, especially in a classroom setting. However, the butterfly attention of an ADHD brain can generate some very fruitful ideas. Invite an ADHD brain into your brainstorming session or workshop and you'll get a barrage of ideas. You just need to be able to jot them down fast enough.

Hyperactivity and impulsivity are also expressed in other types of ADHD, each time to different degrees. Hyperactivity is due to the low number of receptors in the brain compared to a 'normal' person. To put it simply, people with ADHD need twice as many stimuli to produce the same effect. So they're always on the lookout for new stimuli to raise or maintain their dopamine levels. By stimuli, we don't mean a single needle in your brain, but a whole cactus-full. If you have ADHD, you can't sit still, you can't listen, you struggle literally and figuratively to stay on task. Time and again you seek out risky situations. This kick-seeking can be taken to extremes. When our house painter heard that a pair of seagulls had built a nest on the roof, he offered to take a look. He had already figured out that he could use the neighbour's roof to access ours, a nice sloping gable roof, four floors above the ground. Wasn't that dangerous? I asked. He responded dryly: 'Of course it's dangerous, but I need that. Do you understand?' I did, and I nodded. He said he also wanted to find out if seagulls really attack you or just threaten to. My wife and I thought briefly about trying to stop him, but it would probably have been pointless. I nodded again to confirm that I understood.

In many cases, this physical hyperactivity will lessen with age, but turns into even greater mental agitation. For those around them, people with ADHD are not always a gift, to put it mildly. They are sometimes classed as 'difficult', 'hard work' or 'exhausting'. If it's any consolation to those around me: at times I tire myself out too. In slightly more neutral or positive terms, they are sometimes described as having a head full of fireworks. A successful person with ADHD may be labelled as an *enfant terrible*; from the French, meaning 'terrible child', though nowadays it has more of a positive connotation.

The impulsive nature of people with ADHD can be attributed to the different way in which the frontal cortex functions, leading to poor inhibition of thoughts, feelings and behaviour. Blabbermouths indeed. With poor impulse control.

An inability to sit still and a wandering mind are usually seen as traits that get in the way of success. But they can also be the path towards it.

## Where are you on the continuum?

ASD talks about a spectrum and ADHD about a continuum. In both cases, it's a matter of degrees. The line between 'normal' and 'abnormal' is in fact wholly arbitrary. It's the person affected, or the people close to them, who decide whether something is normal or abnormal. Sometimes a person considers themself abnormal and those around them do not, or vice versa. Take anorexia, for example, where a person's self-image doesn't match what those around them see. Despite being extremely underweight, they will still perceive themselves as overweight.

It's about discovering where the extremes lie, and where that puts you on the spectrum. You could liken it to a mixing desk with various parameters ranging from 0 to 10. God is indeed a DJ, as British dance act Faithless put it in the nineties, because he gave each of us our own mixing desk. Observe yourself; self-knowledge is a key step towards identifying your talents. Get others to observe you as well. Your friends, family and ex-teachers will know what you were good at and be able to tell you. Mostly by saying what you were bad at. It's up to you to translate that and score it between -10 and +10 on your mixing desk.

Do you recognize these traits in yourself? They have to do with hyperactivity and ability to concentrate.

- ☐ I need constant movement.
- ☐ I find it hard to wait my turn.
- ☐ I am tireless compared to others.
- ☐ I blurt things out.
- ☐ I'm not one for details.
- ☐ I'm easily distracted.
- ☐ I prefer short-term tasks with lots of variety.
- ☐ I'm sometimes told I have talent, but that it doesn't come out.

If you want to explore a suspected diagnosis of ADHD, there are plenty of questionnaires online. They are not always scientific but do give an indication. I myself don't have an official ADHD diagnosis but, after taking three different online tests, I clearly score quite high on ADHD symptoms, especially the combination of concentration problems and hyperactivity. One of these self-tests also produced the following verdict: 'You seem to cope well with the traits you exhibit.' That is true, though it took me a long time to find a solution to my procrastination. It was my wife who saw to that. This book had been at the back of my mind for several years, but would fade away and come back and, because so much work was involved, I never really got down to it. My wife Emily, a coach herself, suggested drawing up a weekly schedule with lists of priorities. That's certainly one good way to stop being distracted. She also recommended setting clear goals. In my case, that meant writing three pages a week.

It worked! The insurmountable task of writing a book suddenly became manageable. The schedule made me stick to the plan. And that's not easy, because someone with ADHD is prone to believing that the next idea might be a better one. So you keep springing around like a grasshopper in your own mind. What a relief that schedule was. Finally, I was able to continue writing.

## In what work environment do you thrive best?

If you have ADHD, it's hard to choose a single path because you are interested in many different things and you also need variety. You can aim for a single path, but that path needs to carry a lot of diversity. The same goes for your workplace. Here too, it's hard to commit to one place because you find it difficult to sit still. Again, you can aim for a job that offers precisely the freedom you need to go wherever you want and also work the hours you want. Or maybe you'd be better combining two different part-time jobs? Whatever the case, if someone forces you to be somewhere from 9 to 5, you will feel trapped. When you're set free, you'll happily work from 5 to 9 instead of 9 to 5. Simply because you set the pace. Or rather, it's not you setting the pace, but your ADHD.

Without sufficient self-knowledge, it can take decades to find the 'job of a lifetime' through trial and error. With that knowledge, you can find the right job much faster. And that starts with two basic insights from the paragraph above: a single path with different challenges and a single workplace that serves as a base camp for excursions to other locations. People with ADHD love having occasional travel time in their schedule. It brings variety. It means dopamine. It keeps the brain alert. By the way, this travel time needn't always be taken literally. It can also be travelling from project to project in your mind.

'If I'd known all of that sooner, I might not have chosen translation and interpreting for my Master's,' says Elise Cordaro in her testimony. After a degree in journalism, she went on to study Russian but clearly wasn't cut out for translation. She was too easily distracted. 'I'd sit and leaf through a dictionary, having long since forgotten which word I was supposed to be looking up,' she says. And the 'interpreter' part didn't prove a key to success either; constantly listening to someone was just too dull for her ADHD brain.

**Work environments that will keep you happy:**

1. **No permanent desk, but a nomadic existence.** A job where you're not tied to a single desk will make you happy. It will help if you have the freedom to travel to physical meetings with clients or colleagues. A job as a freelancer may also appeal to you, as you'll never be tied to one client or one place for too long. If the work content is not stimulating enough, you'll become restless and soon lose interest.
2. **No routine, but deadlines.** Routine jobs with a predictable pattern are deadly for someone with ADHD. You'll only become restless: clock-watching and miserable due to a lack of

dopamine. You'll fare better in a work environment with deadlines that are not too far ahead. Your procrastination demands deadlines. Think about that.

3. **No 9 to 5, but 24/7.** People with ADHD can be 'in the zone'. If a topic really interests them, they'll stay longer at work, get up earlier, pull an all-nighter. But that hyperfocus will only happen if the topic really grabs them. An employer can tell straight away whether or not someone with ADHD is on board. Either they're invisible or they won't leave you alone.

Of course, it's not just about diversity in your work, it's also about the right colleagues and an understanding environment. We cover this in more detail in Chapter 12 on the importance of environment to neurodivergent people. To touch on it briefly here, I'd like to mention my former fellow student Nathalie. She has never had a diagnosis of ADHD, though it is suggested by a glance at her career path: starting out as a researcher for TV shows, she later became a journalist and editor of several magazines, then set herself up as a tour guide in Istanbul and Los Angeles. During the process of writing this book, I asked her if she had ADHD and, although she denied having it, she did acknowledge that many people believed she had the condition. Furthermore, throughout her career, she has received numerous complaints or comments about her behaviour being 'hyperkinetic'. At a recent job interview she was asked what kind of colleague she would work with best. Her response: 'Someone calm and quiet, the opposite of me.'

A nice illustration of the importance of having the right people around you if you're to unleash your ADHD talents. Understanding colleagues are not a luxury, but a necessity. After all, the fact that you are always hyperactive and restless and have trouble listening can be quite irritating for colleagues. Since I am quite restless myself, Nathalie's restlessness never bothered me. A major advantage is that, at the age of 55, she still claims to have tons of energy. 'I can do much more than people my age,' she says. You might say that ADHD keeps you forever young.

You are
a born crisis
manager.
And if there
isn't a crisis,
you create
one yourself

# What jobs can you excel in?

With an ADHD brain, a career as a professional job hopper might seem obvious. But that's not necessarily your fate. Not if you can find a job that keeps your attention sufficiently on the hop. Or if you can do more than one job at the same time (people with the 'H' in ADHD usually have more than enough energy for that).

My mission is to help you find a vocation where you can fully immerse yourself without feeling the need to take on additional tasks or constantly switch jobs. By choosing a field of work that can gratefully put your 'attention hopping' to use, you turn your disadvantage into an advantage. Below are some schools of thought. Remember, there are many more jobs out there than we can even imagine. And new ones are added every day. Before you read on, let me just say that people with ADHD and a strong 'H' trait are already an asset to any business due to their high energy.

## Jobs for the non-linear thinker

One idea leads to another with you. Take notes, because every thought vanishes as quickly as it came. Make sure you have someone to follow up on your ideas, because people with ADHD are often less good at that. Being ad rem is your best friend. That's why I like to invite my colleague Jef, who you met earlier, to brainstorming sessions. Add a touch of impulsivity and it'll take you a long, long way. People with ADHD have enough going on in their own brains to keep themselves and others busy. Potentially interesting jobs that match this profile are:

→ Creative or concept creator in the communication sector
→ Entrepreneur
→ Stand-up comedian
→ Actor
→ Photographer
→ Architect

## Jobs for the restless soul

You're always on the lookout for a kick. You always need a project, a deadline, a crisis, a challenge, a situation where you can prove yourself. These situations are the antidote to your procrastination, you need them to spur you into action, you need them to calm your mind. Some jobs that fit this profile:

→ Journalist
→ Emergency physician
→ Travel guide
→ Stunt performer
→ Athlete
→ Paramedic
→ Estate agent
→ Actor
→ Gamer

## Jobs for the multitasker

If you have the right mix of ADHD traits, you are destined to start or lead a business. However, you must possess the following characteristics: multitasking abilities, immense resistance, a restless soul that seeks new impulses, a risk-taker, and socially engaging. The latter is crucial to motivate others to contribute to your business, and to find structured finishers who can run a marathon after you've taken the first sprint. Typically, a finisher is a calm but determined force that reminds you to complete half-finished tasks or prevent you from dropping them over the fence to employees who cannot keep up. If you are lucky enough to have these traits, these jobs may be suitable for you:

→ CEO/entrepreneur
→ Politician
→ Investment banker
→ Lawyer
→ Restaurateur or hotel owner

## Note this down before you forget

ADHD individuals are so volatile in their brain that they are constantly seeking the next thrill. When you are focused on something, you can concentrate extremely well, but when you are not actively engaged in a task, your thoughts bounce all over the place. And so do you, as you usually follow those thoughts.

Therefore, if something comes along that gives you a rush, write it down. Otherwise, it will pass and be forgotten.

## To sum up

As with ASD, there is a formula that might help you towards professional success:

Variety + Deadlines + Unrestricted work environment =
PROFESSIONAL SUCCESS

An unrestricted work environment means you should be free to work where and when you want. You need diversity in terms of work content to keep up your dopamine, and you need deadlines in order to perform. But most of all, you need a calm, determined force by your side to make sure you cross the finish line.

A great example of this is Michael Phelps, a swimmer described by many as the G.O.A.T. (Greatest Of All Time). His unusual physique helped, of course, but so did the fact that his ADHD took him to swimming lessons at the age of nine to develop concentration and self-discipline. Today, Phelps is an advocate for mental well-being, having fallen into a black hole like many other athletes after his extraordinarily successful career.

**Alemsah Ozturk, CEO of AKQA Group Turkey**

*ADHD*

———

The fact that Alemsah is somewhere on the ADHD spectrum is clear just from looking at his LinkedIn profile: he is a CEO, start-up mentor, keynote speaker and business angel.

'So much for my professional life, I'm also a social influencer with 300,000 followers and heavily into poetry. But I must admit I envy people who write books, because my ADHD doesn't let me. I never get beyond the length of a poem before I have to start again on something else.

But I still see my ADHD as my superpower. Over time, I've learned to shift my lack of focus on one particular subject to a focus on multiple subjects at the same time. Thanks to my ADHD,

I can manage an almost unlimited to-do list; I jump from one thing to another and my quick mental reactions allow me to make split-second decisions. I create a micro-focus, in a sense, for each micro-task. I'm not bothered by people coming into my office every five minutes, or by unexpected phone calls and occasional WhatsApps. And then of course there's the social side. I can be very social, and someone with ADHD is precisely the sort of person you want at your party.

It's true it did take me a while to learn to accept myself as I am. I had to find out for myself that I had ADHD. In high school, my teachers complained that I had no focus and showed no interest in anything. ADHD wasn't really known of at that time in Turkey. So I booked myself some doctor's appointments. When it turned out I had a mild form of ADHD, I started to read more about it because I wanted to know how to fix it. But it didn't take me long to come to terms with it. By accepting your deficits and beginning to see them as advantages, you turn the whole game board around – and your life too.

Even today, people still think I'm not listening. Which isn't true, I'm just not very good at concentrating. People also think I'm lazy because I can't study for very long. They always think I put things off, but they should know all the stuff going on in my head. Oh well, I've learned to live with that, but it's not pleasant when someone thinks I forget a meeting out of indifference. I forget simply because I forget, you shouldn't read anything more into it. In retrospect, my choice of the communications industry was decided by my ADHD. It's the dream industry for someone with ADHD: you jump from project to project, time and again you're challenged to solve problems, always different ones for different clients in different industries.

Support from your social network is super important. The people around me are already used to my behaviour. For example, they know I get bored quickly if a conversation stalls for too long on one topic. I want to be on a rollercoaster. And if you enjoy that too, then we're a good fit.'

# Chapter 8
## Dyslexia

Dyslexia, like ASD and ADHD, comes in different types and degrees. The way in which a person experiences their dyslexia can also vary. By the way, they could have found an easier word to write or read than dyslexia. And a more flattering description, because dyslexia comes from Greek and literally means 'bad with words'. That's a bit too simplistic. But let's get back to the degrees. It can also be the case that you don't quite have enough characteristics to receive a diagnosis but have enough symptoms to draw talent from it.

Dyslexia is one of the more stigmatizing conditions. If you have ASD or ADHD, you used to be labelled as stubborn or unmanageable. With dyslexia, you were labelled as stupid. Totally unjustified, of course, but this prejudice is part of our society in which reading and writing have gained a certain status. I'm pleased to say that a great deal has changed over the past twenty years, but people with dyslexia are still at risk of being seen as stupid. Our whole education system and society is built on the written word. The use of emojis on social media is perhaps a breath of fresh air, and the Ancient Egyptians with their hieroglyphs were probably dyslexia-friendly as well. But unfortunately, as long as books and courses are not written or filmed in visual language, we'll just have to put up with words made up of characters and deal with the associated difficulties.

Research shows that dyslexia is often associated with ADD or highly variable attention, sometimes accompanied by hyperfocus. That absent-minded professor you see in comic strips failing to find the right word and coming out with crazy malapropisms: he too might be dyslexic.

According to Dr Thomas Armstrong, most people with dyslexia score average or above-average on intelligence tests, though I should immediately qualify this by saying that people with low IQs are not usually tested for this condition. Dyslexia does occur at every level of intelligence, but there is still a strong stigma around dyslexia and people with it are still too often dismissed as not very intelligent.

Fortunately, there are dozens of examples of public figures with dyslexia, proof that this condition need not stand in the way of success. I mentioned Virgin boss Richard Branson earlier, but pop art's Andy Warhol, singer Cher and artists Auguste Rodin, Picasso and Robert Rauschenberg are also thought to be on the dyslexia continuum, as are the famous writers Roald Dahl and Agatha Christie.

Perhaps you too have dyslexic traits, however mild. Which may be a blessing, because dyslexia makes you better in certain areas, which in turn can help in your choice of job. Dyslexia can be the difference between reading a story aloud or making one up. This happens every night in a family in our circle of friends. The non-dyslexic mum reads their son's bedtime story exactly as it is written on the page. The dad, who does have dyslexia, selects an appealing illustration in the same book and makes up his own story to accompany it. Reading the text takes too much effort, but that doesn't stop him weaving fantastic tales around the pictures, and their son is just as happy.

## What is dyslexia?

Dyslexia is a learning disability that manifests in reading and/or writing difficulties. Automatization of reading and/or spelling at word level progresses slowly, and letter and word recognition often remains difficult despite enormous effort.

The reading process involves both decoding (deciphering words and syllables) and word recognition. These two sub-processes are normally performed fluently and almost unconsciously, but not in people with dyslexia. This can lead to slow and hesitant reading, where understanding the content becomes secondary and recognising sounds is difficult. You might read much more slowly than other people, or you might read too fast and guess the words instead of reading them. This 'guessing strategy' leads to incorrect guesses. Learning to recognize individual sounds (or 'phonemes') in words is essential in dyslexia, in order to learn how to translate speech into syllables and eventually into words. Dyslexic people therefore need support in learning how to handle syllables, interpret sounds and connect letters with sounds. During your studies, it's helpful to get accommodations such as additional time to finish exams, syllabi presented as audiobooks instead of written text, and oral exams whenever possible. When people with dyslexia use text-to-speech software, they often perform just as well as others on reading comprehension. The energy freed up allows them to focus on the content and its processing.

In response to these obstacles in terms of letter and word recognition, people with dyslexia will often develop visual creativity. This is an added challenge in our verbal world, though it can also mean they develop a visual talent. And precisely because they have problems finding words, they often have a rich vocabulary. If they can't bring a word to mind, they need to describe it by association or find another word for it. It sounds contra-intuitive, but this coping mechanism allows you to excel even as a translator or interpreter. Toon Cox, now a researcher at KU Leuven and an assistant professor at Vrije Universiteit Brussel, is a good example. Though he says he could never have succeeded without a computer with an autocorrect function.

Dyslexia and talent in the same sentence: it *is* possible! Every disadvantage has a corresponding advantage: because dyslexics think less in words, they are forced to think and remember more in pictures and patterns. So they are more likely to develop holistic perception and visual or spatial skills. They learn to think outside the box and often have many additional unconventional talents, such as an ability to grasp the core or essence of things or the broader context behind a situation or idea. Incidentally, some of them draw on this strength to take a completely different approach to learning to read, focusing on the whole 'word picture' rather than on the sound.

Dyslexia experts Brock and Fernette Eide describe the skill of combining existing things in new ways as an 'inventor's ability'. Dyslexic brains sometimes 'see' interesting associations and relationships more easily.

In a nutshell: dyslexic brains have both different strengths and different weaknesses to 'normal' brains. For example, most people with dyslexia have a fairly limited working memory. They don't retain sounds, numbers, names, times or other facts very readily. But they often do have a good associative memory. Using association, they can develop lots of ideas and often have an unexpected angle on everyday occurrences. So they are often creative problem solvers.

Hopefully it should be clear by now that dyslexia has nothing to do with intelligence. People with dyslexia are no less gifted than others; they are just more likely to have problems in education due to their learning difficulty. In childhood, this may mean you have less time for social contact or hobbies because simply following the ordinary school curriculum demands a huge amount of time and energy. Under-performing in the early school years on simple tasks such as recognizing or writing letters and reading simple words is enormously confusing for a child. They compare themselves to their classmates and don't understand why they can't 'keep up'. Parents and teachers are quick to become frustrated, thinking they're 'a clever child who is probably not trying hard enough'. The extra effort and practice don't ultimately translate into successful progress, according to Anny Cooreman, director of the Eureka school for children with dyslexia/dyscalculia. In the long term this can lead to lower self-confidence, fear of failure, motivation issues or poorer performance in school. This is precisely why it's so important for parents and schools to pick up on the right signals in time and address them. Even for adults, it can still be confronting that other people seem to look down on you because you can't write without making mistakes.

As with autism, dyslexia was long thought to be more common in boys than in girls, but that turns out not to be true. Dyslexia is currently estimated to affect around 5% to 7% of the population. And it often comes with other conditions such as dyscalculia, ADHD or ASD. Because dyslexia is not always hereditary and remains largely unexplored, it is still a common subject of debate, and of scientific research. The key thing to remember is that dyslexic brains function differently to non-dyslexic brains, which doesn't imply that they function any less. An important nuance, if you ask me. Humanity needs a wide range of individual differences: people who are good at fine detail and consistency, but equally others who are more mindful of the bigger picture, of form, context and the underlying goal.

## Where are you on the spectrum?

Everyone has that one tricky word they can't write or read. For me, it's 'gynaecologist' (with thanks to my proof-reader for the correction). It's as if a word has been ironed into your visual memory like a misplaced crease and every time you come to write that word again, you spell it wrong again. There are also some words I have trouble pronouncing. But over the years I have built up a huge arsenal of synonyms, descriptions and metaphors in order to avoid them. Generally, however, my dyslexia is extremely mild, much milder than my ASD (which is most evident) or my ADHD. Though I do feel my very mild dyslexia gives me certain advantages, for example in visualization.

Dyslexia can be diagnosed only after ruling out other causes of reading and writing difficulties (such as hearing problems) and following multidisciplinary diagnostic testing and practical research. But how do you know if you do have a touch – or a wallop – of dyslexia without having to go through that entire process? It depends on whether you can experience its benefits as well.

The following simple questions may help:

- ☐ Do you have words that you struggle to read or write? Do you notice you can't read even a simple children's book without making mistakes?
- ☐ Do you think of yourself as a not-very-good reader? Or did they used to tell you at school that you weren't a good reader because you were slower and more hesitant than other children?
- ☐ Do you sometimes catch yourself being led astray by a reading error that has nothing to do with the original intention of the text?
- ☐ Do you find it difficult to express yourself in writing?

- ❑ Do you avoid reading aloud?
- ❑ Do you struggle to get a feel for numbers or calculations?
- ❑ Does someone in your family have dyslexia? If a family member is dyslexic, you may be too, because dyslexia is 40% to 60% genetic. This is currently a hot topic of scientific research.

What advantages can this offer now? Not many at school, unfortunately – we have to be honest about that. But once out of that setting, you usually get more room to develop your talents and then become good or even excellent at them. And then your dyslexia may be an added bonus: precisely as a result of your condition and the associated problems in education, you may have gradually built up vast reserves of perseverance to prove you still have a lot going for you. You have learned to stand up for yourself and can think in a solution-focused way. You have learned to think more associatively and creatively and are more likely to see the bigger picture.

This is perfectly illustrated by Benjamin Braun, the Chief Marketing Officer of Samsung Europe. In an article in business magazine *Campaign*, he says that he writes his work notes in his native Swedish. Not because he doesn't have a good command of English, but because he is dyslexic: 'I am still embarrassed by my unfortunate spelling. My Swedish spelling is also rubbish, but at least most people at work don't know that. They just see neat handwriting and drawings.' In the same article Braun also explains how his dyslexia helped him shape his career. Seeing the bigger picture helps him in his current job: 'My brain does not seem to bother about the micro as it races to think about the macro. In my role, it helps to be able to have a big vision for where we want to be.' Overall, Braun believes that dyslexia should be seen as a strength, rather than a weakness. He emphasizes that people with dyslexia and neurodivergent people in general have unique skills and perspectives that can be incredibly valuable in the workplace.

## In what work environment do you thrive best?

For dyslexia too, I'd like to give some tips on how to frame yourself properly in a professional context. First of all, it's important to have the necessary freedom in your work environment. You enjoy working independently and in your own way, because that's how you pulled yourself up by your bootstraps in school. You prefer to focus on results rather than on methods (see Eide & Eide, *The Dyslexic Advantage*, 2011). Jobs that allow flexibility, therefore, open the doors to success for people who identify with the dyslexic spectrum. You look for innovative ways to save time, effort and money that will ultimately benefit everyone. Learning expert Dr Angela Fawcett says: 'I think one of the benefits that dyslectics experience from their difficulty mastering procedures is that they have to rethink tasks each time, starting from fundamental principles, instead of having the steps entirely automated and ready to be performed without thinking. Because they can't rely on these automatic skills in a mindless fashion, they're not limited by the rules, so they can think *outside* the rules.'

You enjoy challenging others to question the status quo, as you prefer tackling things differently and more efficiently. Working independently is your preference, which means you don't want a boss who is constantly watching your every move. This kind of flexibility is easy to find in larger organizations, either in senior positions or on the very bottom rung. Or by starting your own business, of course.

Focus is important too, so a quiet work environment is a must. Especially if you recognize yourself in the symptoms of both dyslexia and ADHD. If this is you, noise-cancelling headphones are the best invention ever. (And, of course, they're also useful in reducing external stimuli for people with ASD).

With today's digital tools, individuals with dyslexia or other learning difficulties that affect reading and writing can access a wider range of job opportunities that may have been inaccessible in the past. There is a spellcheck on every imaginable device, you can dictate your emails enabling you to work faster and with ChatGPT you can even generate whole texts. All of these tools are life-changing. But perhaps you've already developed a preference for activities that are more visually oriented.

# What jobs can you excel in?

## Heralds of a new era

Our son is very visually oriented. Combined with his imagination and verbal strengths, this sometimes leads to surprising statements. For example, you can put his dinner on the table and a nanosecond later you'll get the comment: 'Phew, lucky it's fish not prawns, 'cos the prawn's eyeballs will roll down to your belly, and back up to your brain to see what you're thinking.'

When someone says something, do images pop into your mind? Can you picture what a house looks like just from glancing at the floor plan? Can you recall a memory instantly? Then you're a visual thinker too.

Besides imagination, visual thinkers often have good spatial understanding. These strengths are usually offset by problems with arithmetic, which is abstract as opposed to visual. Bill Dreyer, a dyslexic inventor and a biologist at Caltech who was involved in researching the genetic code of protein structures, describes it as follows: 'I think in colourful 3-D Technicolor images instead of words.' His ability to think in pictures is essential to him in developing ground-breaking theories about how antibodies are made and how protein sequences can be replicated. 'I was able to see the machine in my head and rotate valves and actually see the instrumentation,' he says. 'I don't think of dyslexia as a deficiency. It's like having CAD (computer-aided design) in your brain.'

Here are some suggestions for jobs where 3-D thinking is an advantage, as long as you don't have to write long reports about what you do:

→ Film director
→ Cartoon animator
→ Package designer
→ Graphic designer
→ Art director
→ Video editor and VFX artist
→ Interior designer or architect
→ Furniture maker
→ Illustrator
→ Software designer
→ Visual artist
→ Sculptor
→ Choreographer
→ Photographer
→ Cartographer
→ Pilot
→ Camera operator
→ Fashion designer
→ Product developer

According to astrophysicist Larry Smarr, a flaw of the current education system is that scientists are selected based on their analytical skills rather than their visual or holistic abilities. Smarr believes the future of science will become increasingly visual, producing a new generation of scientists who are much more image-oriented. The complex design process for industrial goods, ranging from cars to aircraft engines, will shift to the metaverse (the next iteration of the internet, linking shared physical and 3D virtual spaces in an all-encompassing virtual universe). New forms of collaboration will emerge. For example, an aircraft will be assembled by experts working from different locations, running joint simulations to get the job done. The same goes for education and healthcare. Surgeons can already perform operations remotely from anywhere in the world using VR headsets. Digital disruption can be expected in many sectors. Based on these observations, we have added the following occupations to the list:

→ Physicist
→ Surgeon
→ Radiologist
→ Surveyor
→ Engineer
→ Urban planner


## Outside-the-box entrepreneurs

Not everyone has their sights set on the artistic or scientific world, of course. If you think you're on the dyslexia spectrum, there is a whole range of other career paths open to you. It's not just artists or scientists who can benefit from changes in technology: so can creatives who can see the bigger picture and not lose themselves in details. We are talking here about entrepreneurs who can position themselves in ways that give them a competitive advantage thanks to new trends and economic developments.

Julie Logan, a professor at the Cass Business School in London, looked at the proportion of dyslexic people in entrepreneurial roles versus corporate manager roles. The figures turn out to be 35% versus 1%. Logan believes that dyslexic people have such strong entrepreneurial skills because they had to overcome so many obstacles at school and in their early development. But there are also innate skills linked to this outside-the-box thinking. Billionaire Richard Branson, for example, uses his imagination to devise business plans. He is useless with figures and spreadsheets, but achieves by looking at the bigger picture. Of course, his above-average emotional intelligence has also played a role: it's much easier to motivate others if you have excellent social skills. As he puts it himself in a documentary on dyslexia: 'I think it helps me because I know that I'm not perfect at everything and I find people who are better than me to work with and people with different skills.'

Individuals with dyslexia can excel thanks to their 'big-picture thinking' – even if, like Branson, they need a metaphor to remember the difference between net and gross profit. Branson was 50 before he learned the difference, thanks to a frustrated CFO after yet another board meeting: 'When you go fishing, the fish caught in the net are your net profit. The rest don't count.'

Job options in this category are:

→ CEO/entrepreneur
→ IT coordinator
→ Inventor
→ Consultant
→ Business coach

On an important side note from *The Dyslexic Advantage*, jobs that rely on fine details, routine automated procedures or memory-oriented tasks are less suitable for people on the dyslexia spectrum. Jobs involving a lot of repetition, consistency, attention to detail, procedures or routine are not the best match.

## To sum up

For dyslexia too, I have in mind a formula for success and happiness in the workplace, and it looks like this:

Special interest + Autonomy + Visual gift =
PROFESSIONAL SUCCESS

Special interest refers to the fact that it's best to have both an intrinsic and an extrinsic interest in your job. You might think that's true for everyone, but people with dyslexia depend on their area of interest even more than others in order to give of their best, as scientists Brock and Fernette Eide confirm. In the worst scenario, if a task doesn't interest them, it is very difficult to perform well and stay focused. This special interest should be intrinsic in terms of job content, and also extrinsic – meaning it can lead to interesting things such as money, status or the fulfilment of personal goals. Richard Branson is a living testimony to this. His quote on the topic speaks for itself: 'I set out to create something I enjoyed that paid the bills.'

Autonomy refers to the fact that you like to work independently of others and you define your own outlines and structures. The visual gift is your inherent talent to shape these structures, provided you have actually given this talent the attention it needs in order to flourish. Your work environment should not be over-stimulating, so you can focus enough to find your way through these structures. Your perseverance comes into its own in a context like this.

Steven Spielberg, the successful American director and producer, is a perfect example to back up this formula. Spielberg had a huge influence on the film industry through his talent for turning simple tales into spectacular cinematic events with stunning special effects, strong storytelling and bombastic scores. He achieved this professional success despite a difficult educational career that held little interest for him. To be a successful filmmaker, it's essential to have a strong vision that stems from your passion. You must be able to stand by your vision, even if sponsors try to alter your script. Additionally, you need to possess undeniable visual talent. On set, focus is crucial to delivering a successful production, which can be achieved with a well-coordinated production team that brings your artistic vision to life. Spielberg did not receive his dyslexia diagnosis until the age of 60. Luckily, he had already focused on his visual talent well before that.

**Regula Ysewijn, author of six books, culinary historian and judge for the Platinum Pudding Competition, featured in a special BBC documentary.**
*Dyslexia and dyscalculia*

———

'I'm proud to say today that I have dyslexia and dyscalculia, as if they're my battle scars in life. As a girl, I had to spend hours writing out numbers in the right sequence under the dreaded eye of the nuns. I thought I was being punished. Not a week went by without stomach aches and nerves about tests. But when I was ten I wrote my first short story, which I promptly dressed up with a cardboard binding and a cover illustration. I turned out to have a keen interest in history, art and mythology, which soon created an expectation in my parents that I would continue in mainstream secondary education. Art school was out of the question.

I could only meet those expectations in the subjects of history and art. My interest in history then evolved into a fascination with British culture. I learned English from Jane Austen novels, a tattered English dictionary and the BBC, and I began writing stories in English. I noticed that English flowed out of me naturally in a way that Dutch did not.

In mainstream education meanwhile, results failed to materialise. So I ended up in a vocational stream where I did graphic design and illustration; this was where the school system put just about every creative it didn't know what to do with.

I achieved fantastic results but, however good they were, they didn't give me the opportunity for further study. Evening classes seemed to be the only option to fulfil my dream. I was already living on my own, going out to work, and studying in the evenings and at weekends. Unfortunately, I became unwell due to lack of sleep and a varied diet, so I had to drop my evening classes. I only had enough energy to work to pay my rent. With no degree but a drive to succeed, I decided to look for a job as a graphic designer. I convinced advertising agencies to give me a chance and was given assignments which I managed and carried out myself. In the space of a year I worked my way up from intern to senior. When I felt I wanted more on the creative side, I launched a website about British food and history, and it took off. Soon I was getting requests for photography and began writing a column on the culinary history of England in a British culinary magazine and an online publication. Shortly after, I resigned from my graphic design job and at a publisher's request wrote my first book Pride and Pudding on the history of British puddings accompanied by recipes. I did the design and photography myself and my husband did the illustrations. The book was selected for the Great British Food Awards and the National Trust asked me to write a book on the subject for them as well. The fact that I'm not British wasn't an issue for them. My lack of a degree, even less so.

Four more books followed. No one saw the limitations of my dyslexia and dyscalculia, or the stigma of "no degree". People only saw my achievements. Hard-earned proof. By 2021, I was one of the best-selling culinary authors in Britain. I also broke through in America and my latest book was nominated as one of the best books of the year by The New Yorker and The Washington Post.

I am self-made, self-taught, but above all tenacious. The outdated school system and the negligence in diagnosing my dyscalculia and dyslexia taught me from a young age what it means to struggle yet keep on steadfastly believing in yourself.

Yes, I have moments of insecurity, and I've had setbacks, but you have to turn them into motivation. Because if there's one thing I've always believed in and want to impress on others, it's that you need to do everything you can to make your dreams come true and that hard work is the key to everything.'

# Today I am proud to say I have dyslexia and dyscalculia

# A desire for completeness

# Chapter 9
# Obsessive-compulsive disorder (OCD)

## What is OCD?

In the opening scene of *As Good As It Gets*, when Jack Nicholson hurls his neighbour's dog down the garbage chute of his apartment building, checks the lock on his front door three times, turns the hallway light on and off three times, takes one of forty bars of soap from the bathroom cabinet and drops it in the bin after a single use, everyone knows that something's not right.

Obsessive-compulsive disorder (OCD) is among the most fascinating of the psychiatric conditions: bizarre but understandable, normal but abnormal. This film example depicts OCD in an extreme form I wouldn't wish on anyone. There are also many other subtypes of OCD, such as 'harm OCD' which involves intrusive thoughts about violent behaviour (fortunately people with OCD never act on these unpleasant thoughts), or 'sexual orientation OCD', where people are plagued by obsessive, completely unfounded doubts about their sexuality. Another unwelcome behaviour related to OCD is trichotillomania or 'trich', in which people pull out their own hair. In a much milder form, some people also have a fear of germs, a fear that was especially triggered during the COVID pandemic. I'll never forget my wife going shopping at the local supermarket wearing ski goggles and a home-made mask fashioned from an old bra. Yes, she too is on the left of a spectrum, where a condition doesn't present as a disorder but can still be quite annoying.

OCD can manifest in many ways and to varying degrees. Looking around at my circle of acquaintances, I can see quite a few mild cases: one of my best friends, for example, only trusts numbers that are divisible by three. Otherwise all hell can break loose. My father has a compulsive ritual when eating apples: he slices the apple with a kitchen knife and then picks it up with the knife slice by slice, starting with the bottom one. This is the only way he can eat an apple, probably afraid of finding a worm in his afternoon snack. A colleague of mine always takes the same route to the station. One day, when his route was blocked by a pile of backpacks dropped by some waiting students, he simply walked across the top of them, because that was the route he *had* to take.

Compulsive thoughts and behaviours manifest not only in anxieties, but also in rituals and superstitions. Many athletes are superstitious, which makes them a bit compulsive in their behaviour. Indeed, people are more superstitious if the situation or outcome is unpredictable. In the world of football (or 'soccer' as it's known in the US), Johan Cruijff springs to mind. Before a match, the Ajax player liked to spit his chewing gum out on the opposing team's half of the pitch. He forgot to do it once, during the 1969 European Cup final against AC Milan. You can guess what happened next: Ajax lost 4-1. Another superstition involved his shirt number. Ever since 30 October 1970, Cruijff always wore the number 14. This came about by chance when, after an extended absence due to a groin injury, he found his usual number 9 shirt had been taken by Gerrie Mühren. Cruijff picked up a spare number 14 and Ajax went on to win against PSV Eindhoven. The rest is history: shirt number 14 and Cruijff became synonymous. Research by Prof. Dr Michaéla Schippers found that 80% of elite athletes (including footballers, hockey players and volleyballers) perform superstitious actions before competing. Eating four pancakes beforehand, peeing in your football shorts or a range of other activities can supposedly do wonders for the outcome of the game.

Sometimes it's done purely out of superstition, a magic charm. Tennis seems to be one of these sports that is full of ritualistic movements. In the case of top Spanish player Rafael Nadal, experts identified a dozen rituals during a tennis match. USA *Today* counted as many as nineteen. Nadal himself denies having a compulsive disorder: he sees it as a way to get into a mental flow. But some of his repetitive actions are indeed remarkable. When he stands up, he pulls his socks up to the same level. He always has two drinking bottles at the ready, and always in the same position. He takes a sip from both bottles at each change of ends. By the way, in 2014, Czech player Lukáš Rosol tried to poke his opponent's psyche by touching Nadal's water bottles with his racket at a change of ends, so they were no longer perfectly aligned. Compulsive behaviour is also deeply ingrained in many other tennis players. Novak Djokovic shows similar compulsive behaviour, bouncing the ball endlessly before serving, for example. But that is nothing compared to Nadal's dozen or more rituals.

These are all fairly innocuous examples of course, but in reality many people suffer from a genuine disorder manifesting in uncontrollable thoughts, impulses or actions. 'Where good tips over into evil', as psychiatrist and OCD patient Menno Oosterhoff put it so aptly in one conversation with me.

Let me take this opportunity to play a final Roman trump card. This is a good place to pause and talk about my favourite Roman emperor, Julian the Apostate. The 'Apostate' because he was raised as a Catholic in the 4th century AD but rejected Christianity in early adulthood. As a newly minted emperor, he then set out to bring back pagan customs and reopen the temples. For this reason he is regarded as the last pagan Roman Emperor, who made Constantinople his seat of operations. These activities won him his most laudatory epithet: *restaurator templorum* or 'restorer of temples'. But he also had another epithet, a less glorious nickname: 'the butcher'. Julian was so obsessed with sacrifices that he wanted to hold one to mark every occasion and seal every decision. After he visited Antioch in present-day Turkey, the locals expressed their joy that he hadn't stayed any longer, or they would have had no cattle left. His obsession with sacrifice must of course be seen in the context of its time, when omens were everything. If a flock of birds flew by from left to right or right to left, it could make all the difference between a bad outcome or a good one. So his behaviour needs to be seen in context, but even contemporaries described him as someone who was extremely compulsive about sacrifices. His obsession with omens and sacrifices failed to save him, as his empire was only short-lived. Julian's ambition was to undo the power of Christianity but he reigned only from 361 to 363, not long enough to succeed in this mission. When he decided to launch a campaign against the Persians, he ironically ignored all the omens that suggested this act was doomed to failure. Against all better judgment, he decided to wage war anyway. In the heat of battle, he was killed. Or murdered, as suspicions are that the deadly arrow came from within his own ranks. With his assumed OCD and ASD, Julian clearly had a small circle of friends but an even larger group of enemies who turned against him and his vision. Though fair and just, it was also heavily critical: Julian certainly had a laser-sharp focus, but sadly no awareness of causing offence.

It is only relatively recently, in the 1980s, that science has begun to examine OCD and develop effective treatments. In the media on the other hand, OCD quickly became a hot topic and sparked a flurry of wild stories about the condition.

Nowadays OCD is part of our general culture. Many famous figures are believed highly likely to have had OCD. A funny example is actor Leonardo DiCaprio, who once claimed he had to step on every blob of chewing gum on the street. Mathematician John Nash is another famous figure who was known as much for his genius as for his madness and probably had both OCD and schizophrenia. He won the 1994 Nobel Prize for Economics for inventing the Nash equilibrium in game theory, as well as the 2015 Abel Prize in recognition of his mathematical genius. In a strange quirk of fate, Nash died in a car accident while driving back to the airport after the ceremony. A more contemporary example is Elon Musk, the CEO of Tesla and SpaceX. In 2015 Musk said on Twitter (even then his favourite platform): 'I have OCD on product-related issues. I only see what's wrong. I never see what's right.' If this is true, it seems to be a good starting point for wanting to improve things and build a billion-dollar business. People with compulsions are often very conscientious and can handle a lot of work.

But it doesn't have to go that far. Maybe you're reading this chapter out of a healthy curiosity because you have some obsessions or compulsions yourself. Or maybe you're reading this piece and feeling ashamed because you've never dared before to talk about your compulsive behaviour? Whatever the case, we'll look for its benefits, though we don't deny that living with OCD – especially a severe form – is pretty tough. But know that a mild form of OCD, such as a fear of germs, doesn't necessarily get in the way of a working and social life. You needn't be a slave to your condition; you can become its master. As long as your passion doesn't tip over into a compulsion and your condition doesn't disrupt your life.

## Where are you on the spectrum?

First things first, how can you tell if you're somewhere on the OCD spectrum? To get a diagnosis of OCD, you need to have obsessions or compulsions that cause you great distress and also interfere with your social functioning or role fulfilment. 'Obsessions' refers to recurring intrusive thoughts, while 'compulsions' refers to actions you feel compelled to perform. Both deplete your energy. Examples are excessive cleaning, writing things down, checking, organizing, counting – but praying can be a manifestation too. These actions are intended to prevent or rectify an undesirable situation or event, and performing them is demanding or exhausting.

The vicious cycle associated with OCD is called the 'OCD spiral': the compulsion soothes the anxiety in the short term, but in the long term actually reinforces the obsession. So you are drawn deeper and deeper into the spiral.

Recent research in the US shows that as many as two adults in every hundred fall on the spectrum. The cause of OCD has not yet been scientifically proven, but research by Lee Baer, Professor of Psychology at Harvard Medical School, shows that it is partly inherited and is genetically related to other disorders such as agoraphobia, depression, ADHD and Tourette syndrome. Behavioural therapy can be very successful, correcting the brain's overactivity in a matter of weeks. In a sense it soothes the itch in your head, as Menno Oosterhoff puts it. Treatment based on medication is also available.

As you know by now, I'm especially interested in the twilight zone of OCD, where the symptoms are tolerable and confer advantages over people without OCD.

Because OCD comes in many variations and has several subtypes, the questions below should be interpreted as broadly as possible:

☐ Do you have a fear of germs or bacteria, or maybe you're afraid of infecting other people with something? Or in day-to-day life do you constantly worry about non-contagious diseases, such as cancer?

☐ Do you regularly bulk-buy kitchen paper, cleaning products, hand towels or paper handkerchiefs?

☐ Do you perform certain control rituals that involve closing doors, turning off gas stoves, water taps and light switches, or switching off electrical appliances?

☐ Or maybe you have trouble reading, writing, emailing or doing simple sums because you're constantly checking that you haven't made any mistakes?

☐ Do you always do certain actions following the same pattern, or do you repeat actions a set number of times to prevent misfortune from befalling yourself or your family members?

☐ Or do you have to repeat certain phrases when performing specific actions?

☐ Do you feel an urge to count things, such as ceiling tiles or paving slabs?

- Are you superstitious and do you make connections between objects and your superstitions? Maybe you have unlucky times or dates you prefer to avoid? Or do unlucky numbers play a role in your everyday life? This can also extend to unlucky colours.
- Are you afraid to throw away paper, notes or other things because you never know when they might come in handy again?
- Do you have a strong need for symmetry or accuracy?
- Do you spend a lot of time on daily routines?

If you experience any of these symptoms, you'll probably have to admit that they can sometimes be a waste of time or energy. But this needn't be the case if these rituals or actions can be part of your job description. If you have a strong control urge, for example, you could be an airport security guard. No one would smuggle more than 100ml of their expensive face cream onto the plane with you in charge. Fear of germs can be a strength too, if bacteria are indeed the biggest enemy in your workplace, say in an operating theatre. Or if counting is a regular ritual, accompanying children on day trips might be something that appeals to you. Speaking of rituals, it has even been suggested that there are similarities between rituals in extreme orthodox religion and obsessive-compulsive disorder. Freud called it a *Privatreligion* for a reason.

Before trying to find a suitable work environment, it makes sense to get a clear idea of your obsession or compulsion. Check with friends or family and ask what they view as 'normal' behaviour. On that basis, you can work out how pronounced your condition is and where it might give you an advantage. For example, fear can be negative because it paralyzes and makes you vulnerable. But it can also be a strength that lends you a competitive advantage, in the shape of greater productivity or a proactive attitude. For creative people, anxiety or agitation can be a source of inspiration for writing or other forms of artistic expression. It takes you to new ideas and places you'd never think of otherwise. It also makes you aware of possible consequences of decisions, so you can weigh up multiple factors and make more thoughtful choices. This talent comes in handy in certain leadership roles. Strong leaders think before they act.

# In what work environment do you thrive best?

An ideal work environment for you is one where you can be entirely yourself and where you can use your compulsion as a talent. Other people appreciate your obliging nature or proactive attitude, as mentioned above, and accept your different perspective on the world. And by bringing your anxiety out into the open you lighten its burden and may even be able to laugh about it. If you can share these things with those around you, it may help others who may be dealing with similar anxieties. In this way you can help yourself and those around you and support each other, which makes for closer relationships in the workplace. You can also actively seek help in saving you from your own thoroughness, so your passion doesn't turn into a compulsion and overstrain you.

An inclusive work environment that allows for openness and individuality is definitely right for you. But even more comfortable might be a work environment where sharing is not necessary, as you mostly work on your own and can live your passion undisturbed without having to find the patience to delegate certain tasks. Which doesn't mean you can't function in a corporate context. The key point is that you find a place where you can develop your specialism, and that others support you in this by taking on additional or supporting responsibilities that don't compete with your own core task. Colleagues can also be useful in dragging you out of your bubble and guaranteeing a healthy work/life balance.

# What jobs can you excel in?

If you show traits of OCD, you can still excel in your profession, provided that your compulsion does not prevent a normal life. Just like with perfectionism, your performance will improve as your need for control increases, but there is a point of no return after which your performance is overshadowed by your compulsive behaviour. The examples below are intended for people who still have mastery of their obsessions or compulsive behaviours and can use them as a talent.

*Jobs for people with control rituals and/or where long-term projects need to be seen through to completion:*
→ Security guard
→ Forester
→ Detective or investigator
→ Pharmacist
→ Doctor/psychiatrist
→ Nurse
→ Aircraft mechanic
→ Librarian
→ Producer of films or events
→ Childminder
→ Driving instructor
→ Gardener
→ Researcher
→ Food inspector

→ Editor
→ Investigative journalist

*Jobs for people with cleaning rituals:*
→ Beauty therapist
→ Cleaning attendant in a hospital or healthcare facility

*Jobs for people with repetitive rituals and counting compulsions:*
→ Accountant
→ Cashier
→ Lab technician
→ Antiquarian
→ Chef
→ Performance marketer
→ Courier
→ Academic
→ Athlete

## To sum up

For the anxious or compulsive readers among us, I have of course devised a formula that can help you find success in the workplace. In fact, this one is entirely logical:

Specific anxiety + Impact + Inclusive environment = PROFESSIONAL SUCCESS

You start out from the specific anxiety behind your thoughts and/or behaviours, provided it is still controllable, as discussed above. You mustn't lose yourself in your obsessions or compulsive behaviours, but need a certain mastery over them in order to use your OCD as a talent.

Then you look for a job where you can exploit this anxiety and so fulfil the need or desire to protect, preserve or obtain something. As long as you can do this in a work environment that embraces this sensitivity, you'll be fine. But it *is* important to be careful it doesn't fuel your compulsion to such a degree that you lose control over it and slide towards the right on the spectrum. This is why I see 'impact' as part of your formula for success.

The example of Elon Musk came up earlier. The business magnate claims to be concerned about the survival of the human race. From that perspective, he urges us to look at the potential pitfalls of artificial intelligence as well as its benefits: we need to avoid robots taking over power on Earth. He also wants to democratize manned spaceflight, so there would be a way out if this planet goes to pot. His ideas don't seem to have done him any harm, even if they were just a marketing stunt. Musk is currently one of the richest people on Earth. And maybe soon on Mars too.

In stark contrast is the young environmental activist Greta Thunberg, named 'Swedish Woman of the Year' by several bodies and nominated for the Nobel Peace Prize at the tender age of 16 for her efforts to get politicians to reduce $CO_2$ emissions. With a diagnosis of OCD and Asperger syndrome, Greta's motto is 'Being different is a superpower.' Rather than trying to find a new planet, she believes there are no grey areas when it comes to our survival. We either continue as a civilization or we don't. And that also applies to her efforts to convince the world of this.

**Menno Oosterhoff,**
**child and adolescent psychiatrist and writer**
*OCD patient*

———

'As you can see, I do call myself a patient. Because we shouldn't sugar-coat it, it's definitely a burden you suffer. But if you can be and achieve something despite the condition, you deserve all the more respect.

I gradually diagnosed myself, as I'd been slipping further into perfectionism for years. My OCD began when my father became terminally ill and died and, as a result, my perfectionist behaviour of wanting to write everything down was linked with that event and not recognized as OCD. At some point I realized it wasn't down to this event but to the chemistry of my own brain. This was when a patient came to me with identical compulsions but no such experience of loss. It was only while writing my book on compulsion in 2017 that I realized that needing to discuss every aspect of my relationship was another form of compulsion. Then it became even clearer that my passion could spill over into compulsion. It might seem odd, but in many respects OCD was as natural to me as water is to a fish. You're not aware of it yourself.

Not all of my compulsions are entirely useless. OCD gives me an overall drive and a tremendous amount of energy I can put to good use as a psychiatrist and writer. I take on the world eagerly, I do a lot and I want to help every patient who comes to me. I am always on fire. In everything I do – it's like King Midas turning everything into gold – I have to watch it doesn't tip straight over into a compulsion. Because I want to tackle it so thoroughly and precisely. It has sometimes been a reverse realization with me: I knew I was doing something differently from other people. Only afterwards did I realize it was OCD.

Since taking medication (for around twelve years now), my condition has been manageable and I have an even better understanding of how it affects every area of my life. Though I do need to stay alert about not trusting my own intuition. If I deliberately don't tell my wife about a "fun" new research topic, it's probably another compulsion. Then I'll work on it underground for a while until she finds out. I can't always draw the line myself, but happily I have people around me to point it out. I have a partner and children, but in fact I barely have any space for them. I'm not the sort of father who can stand beside a football pitch for hours on end. But I am very fond of them. Fortunately, they are also very fond of me.

My compulsive disorder is part of my identity, I really wouldn't know what I'd be like without my drive. I became a psychiatrist because I wanted to do something for others, my OCD helps me to keep exploring every case and find a solution. It's true that I've always worked alone, that's the environment in which I thrive best. I would hate to have to work too closely with others. Everything has to be done together these days. Luckily I've already retired and no longer have to go along with that trend.

Nowadays I try to do something positive with my condition and use it to benefit others. I'm in the unique position of being able to draw on my own experience as a psychiatrist and patient to help and support others. My ultimate goal is to increase our understanding of mental conditions, so more kindness can emerge. Both from those around them and from the actual patients, who are often very harsh on themselves even though they already have so much to endure. It's a disease, not a decision. The art is being able to see bright spots without denying the darkness.'

It's a disease,
not a decision.
The art is being
able to see the
bright spots

# Chapter 10
## The peach test

For those who don't have time to read the whole book but were triggered by the title, we have added this chapter as a short-cut. Although not a scientific tool, the peach test is a simple and enlightening way to determine if you might be on the neuro-divergent spectrum.

One of the ways we can explore how our brain works is by looking at how different people respond to the same stimulus. That is exactly what we do with the peach test. By trying it out on people with a range of neurodivergent conditions, we've discovered fascinating differences in the way different brains approach the same scenario. As we said, it's not a scientific tool, but it's a creative way to explore the unique and complex ways our brains work.

The test goes as follows:

*Suppose I give you a peach and you can eat it right away. What are your thoughts and feelings on seeing it?*

The following responses give a possible indication of where you might fall on the neurodivergent spectrum.

## Suspected ASD

First I look at the tiny hairs on the peach, especially if the light catches them so they look like blonde hairs on a woman's thigh. They take up so much attention that I have to mentally get over them in order to eat the peach. Then I cut the peach all around with a knife and twist it in two so I can check that the kernel is intact and there are no spiders inside, which happened to me once as a boy, on holiday in the former Yugoslavia. Then I take the kernel out and am ready to enjoy the two halves of my peach.

**Diagnosis:** *Here you can see the attention to detail of a person with ASD, with an added hint of anxiety disorder. In a positive sense, we call it imagination. Also note the exceptional memory.*

## Suspected ADHD

I'll start eating right away without enjoying it. And while eating, I'll think how many more peaches I'll eat after this one. And wonder when the cleaner is coming this week. And if there's any polish left? By now the peach is finished, but I didn't think about how it actually tasted. I wash my hands and pick up a dish towel to dry them. And while I'm at it, I might as well load the dishwasher.

**Diagnosis:** *Here you can clearly see the non-linear, multitasking brain at work. And the crisis manager has been activated even before there's a crisis.*

## Suspected dyslexia

A peach evokes a positive feeling, because I see myself as a child crawling under a fence to pick one from a tree laden with ripe fruit. A peach is calming too, I think due to its softness and pastel skin. It's a touchable fruit, unlike bright red strawberries or a prickly pineapple. A peach has a lovely organic shape, it has an erotic aura around it. Think of the emoji that's taken on a different meaning. You look at it and know exactly how it's going to taste.

**Diagnosis:** *Notice the tendency to focus on the visual aspect and the systemic mindset that automatically compares the peach to other fruits.*

*Someone who is more distrusting, possibly as a secondary consequence of negative reactions from people around them due to a late diagnosis, writes:*

I find this question strange, I'd probably ask a hundred times if I'm allowed to eat it. Why are you giving me this peach? I'll probably mull this over for a while after you've given it to me. It seems highly suspect for you to say 'there's nothing wrong with it, just eat it'. But that's because I assume that if people ask me to do such a thing, it's to make fun of me.

## Suspected OCD

I turn the peach around a few times in every direction to check for bruises or other signs of decay. But I'd still give it back afterwards, because I don't like peaches, they feel a bit too hairy to me...

**Diagnosis:** *Notice here that the object is scanned for abnormalities and is still deemed unsatisfactory. The natural reflex is not to trust the situation, since in any case a peach can never match up to the ideal of a hairless fruit.*

If you recognize yourself from the above descriptions, you can use the diagram below to rate yourself on the spectrum of your disorder(s).

## Where are you on the spectrum?
## Plot yourself on each of the axes below.

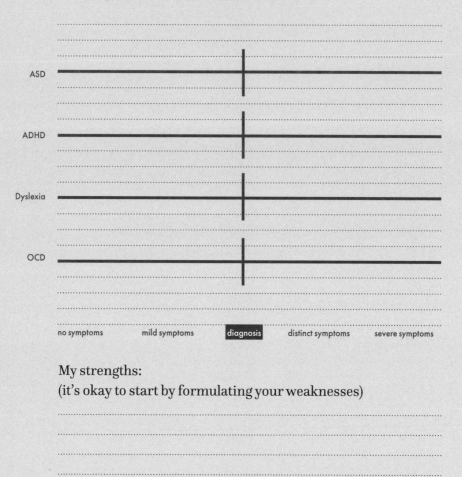

ASD

ADHD

Dyslexia

OCD

no symptoms     mild symptoms     diagnosis     distinct symptoms     severe symptoms

## My strengths:
(it's okay to start by formulating your weaknesses)

# Formulas for professional success

## ASD
Adapted work
environment
+
Unique
interest
+
Special gift

## DYSLEXIA
Special
interest
+
Autonomy
+
Visual
gift

## ADHD
Variety
+
Deadlines
+
Unrestricted
work
environment

## OCD
Specific anxiety
+
Impact
+
Inclusive
environment

# Some plants grow better in the shade

Emily Rammant

# PART III

# Find your biotope

Surround
yourself
with people
who make up
for your
weaknesses
and embrace
your strengths

# Chapter 11
# The importance of the right context

By now, you may have grown more comfortable with the terms 'disorder' or 'condition' and perhaps even developed a newfound appreciation for certain qualities in yourself or your loved ones. From my own experience, I can say that becoming aware of my position on the spectrum has brought me a great deal of self-knowledge. It was a feeling that swung from confrontational to revelatory in a split second. I have gained the ability to not only identify my talents but also discern what brings me joy and what doesn't align with my passions. Just as important as this insight into myself is the huge realization that people on a neurodivergent spectrum are crucially dependent on having the right environment. In the same way that flowers and plants will bloom and grow in different conditions. Some need full sun; others do better in the shade. At the BAM Marketing Congress in May 2022 with the theme *Move with the Times*, I put it like this during my session on *The power of neurodiversity*: 'To flourish, you need to bring together people who embrace each other's strengths and respect or compensate for each other's weaknesses.' This was a call to businesses, but finding the right configuration is important at any time in your life. It starts as a child and being able to grow up with understanding parents. It also applies to finding the right life partner. And in your career as well, having the right colleagues and the right corporate culture will play a crucial role. This may sound surprising, but I never used to believe in myself; I always needed people who believed in me.

The communications industry has always been my natural habitat, yet I felt encouraged and valued by some employers and short-changed and misunderstood by others. Even though the job content was identical. I know now that I don't thrive in a 'you must' environment: you must win awards at the Cannes Lions Festival, you must finish something by tonight, you must report every day, you must attend social events. I cringe at meetings where everyone calls each other 'my friend' from the off. And I can't bring myself to call someone's work 'amazing' if I think it merely ordinary. Luckily, I'm now in a work environment where my neuropsychological traits are taken into account: I *may* win awards, I get freedom to set my own deadlines, and I can decide for myself whether to go to certain industry events. And if I do go, it's okay if I disappear after an hour. Without attracting reproachful comments about the cost of the entry ticket. By the way, my big disappearing act is a running gag in our company. But it does make me feel good mentally and allows me to excel at what I do.

More and more creative and digital industries are recognizing the benefits of neurodivergence. Major corporations such as Amazon, Microsoft, Google and SAP have been working for a number of years on projects in which neurodivergent people can use their talents to find innovative solutions. This becomes even more relevant in the current zeitgeist where, since COV- ID-19, the reality changes every day and new situations call for disruptive solutions. I firmly believe that these changes will come primarily from people on the left or right side of the neurodivergent spectrum.

## Talent alone is not enough

Context is vitally important. In Part II of this book, for each neuropsychological condition, we have therefore added a passage about the biotope in which you thrive best and can come into your own. Because it's not enough to discover your talent, you also need to surround yourself with the right people and find a nurturing culture.

Let's start by taking a look at 'talent'. In his book *Talent is Never Enough*, American author John C. Maxwell lists thirteen factors that determine whether your talent will also lead to success. Strikingly, most of these factors are intrinsic, so Maxwell places the responsibility for developing a talent squarely on the individual. We need to situate this in its time frame: the book was published in 2007, a time when empowerment placed power but also responsibility on the individual. This always reminds me of a legendary campaign headline for the British weekly *The Economist*: 'Having potential is great, if you are 12.' And if you didn't exploit that potential, it was mainly down to you.

Maxwell highlights the importance of intrinsic values such as focus, training, character and perseverance. Something I take no issue with, because I too believe that practice makes perfect. Take attention, for example. Attention is like a muscle you can train. Some people will naturally have a stronger 'attention muscle' than others. A person with ADHD stands at the starting line with a significant disadvantage, but they can take steps forward. Our brains are flexible. You may be familiar with the story of London taxi drivers. Despite the availability of navigation apps, they are still required to undergo two to four years of training until they know all the streets of their city by heart, as well as the fastest route to each destination. If you regularly scan the brain of such a taxi driver, you will see remarkable things happen: the shape of their brain changes and the hippocampus grows larger. This is the region of the brain with the function of storing and retrieving memories.

Our brains can clearly shape themselves to some degree. See also the diagram in the preface, where 'training and compensating' is an important step toward transcending your condition. In this way you experience a dual benefit: you minimize your condition wherever possible, while benefiting from its accompanying gift. Some people find that breathing techniques, meditation or music are effective in training their attention muscle. Others need to write down as much as they can with paper and pen to maintain or prolong their focus. Taking regular breaks is also important. The point is that you can experiment to find out what works for you. We don't of course claim that wherever there's a will, there's a way. Dealing with a mental condition is often a struggle, it demands a lot of you.

But you can't do it all alone. This is where Maxwell falls short, in my opinion. His book devotes only two chapters to the entourage around a person, yet the entourage is incredibly important, especially for people with a neuropsychological talent. Indeed, external factors are essential in order to protect and develop that talent. The employer can play a role in this, as creating employment for people with neurodivergent profiles is currently a major challenge in our society. For example, there is disproportionately high unemployment among people with autism, even those who have above-average levels of education (Riedel et al., 2016). A presentation by Autism-Europe to the European Parliament's Committee on Employment and Social Affairs on 5 November 2019 reported a labour participation rate of under 10% – well below the overall rate of 47% for people with disabilities and 72% for people without disabilities.

James Mahoney, executive director and head of Autism at Work at J.P. Morgan, doesn't mince his words: 'Many people with autism are simply brilliant – highly educated, very capable, with attention to detail, and yet unemployed.' Fortunately, the importance of a healthy mindset and proper framing is growing due to the current trend focusing on inclusiveness. One example is sport, where a shift is clearly perceptible and physical trainers are being paired with coaches trained in psychology. But it's not just elite athletes who need a resilient mindset to achieve peak performance. The same is true for you and me. A safe, supportive and nurturing environment is essential.

In this book, we identify two major influences: people and culture. Starting with people, the next chapter focuses on the role of parents, friends and colleagues. The final chapter looks mainly at corporate culture, where the current focus on inclusiveness and diversity is a positive trend for everyone, including people on a neurodivergent spectrum.

In a professional context, this brings us to three logical steps: know yourself, surround yourself with the right colleagues who embrace your strengths and make up for your weaknesses, and choose a nurturing corporate culture. This is how you get a business or organization with confident individuals, high-performing teams and innovative thinking.

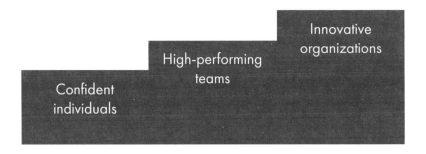

# Chapter 12
## The influence of people

### Life partner and friends

If you're on the spectrum for one or more neurological conditions, it's extremely important to find a partner who sees your way of being as singular rather than peculiar. Speaking for myself, it's only now I'm becoming fully aware of its consequences in a relationship. For example, my partner needs to be aware that I take every question literally and will answer with brutal honesty. My wife knows not to expect an automatic compliment when she asks if her party outfit looks okay. If she asks me that question, she'll get detailed feedback. As a partner, you need to be able to deal with that. Or better yet, turn it to your advantage. In the above scenario, for example, my wife could end up with a nicer outfit. Though I can imagine she would sometimes prefer a less honest answer.

Each neurodivergent condition comes with its own traits, and you need to be able to handle them. People on the autism spectrum can hurt others without meaning to, due to their directness. But they can be hurt easily too. If you shame them for their honesty or point out strange behaviour, they become insecure and withdraw into themselves even more. People with ADHD also like to have a full social life with lots of activities. If your partner is someone who prefers to read books and visit museums, sooner or later you will clash.

In any relationship, it's important to find someone who understands you, believes in you, nurtures, encourages, comforts and pushes you. That seems logical, but look around and you'll notice that not every relationship is made up of partners who give each other positive energy. A crucial factor here is transparency, and ideally naming your condition as early as possible in the relationship. Social commitments, for example, can be a source of contention, as they demand much more energy from you but may actually energize your partner. Discussing this and making arrangements that suit you both can avoid friction and misunderstandings. In this way your partner can support you as effectively as possible.

The same trade-off applies to friends. I always felt different in a social setting, but could never put my finger on it. Let's just say that, in company, I always felt a bit like the *Star Trek* character Mr Spock. Here too, it helps to know that I am on the spectrum. I used to have a compelling urge to isolate myself, and at times I still do. My brain can suddenly say: 'Okay, enough social contact, I'm out of here.' It's important that your friends don't make an issue of this. For me, ideal friends have always been the ones who remain equally close regardless of how often we see each other. And the friends I click with are those who have no expectations of me. One of them once put it like this: 'You know what's so good about our friendship, we don't have to see each other to know that we're there for each other.' I've always remembered these words, because they reassured me and at the same time took the stress out of social commitments. And I'm clearly not the only one: in her interview for this book, Elise Cordaro told me that she too only sees her best friend three times a year.

Please note: I'm definitely not giving myself a free pass to be blissfully insensitive with anyone else. And I don't want to hide behind my condition, or use it as an easy excuse. Nowadays I try to be more conscious of my own feelings, as well as those of others. For example, I used to be able to just drop out of a friendship – without warning – and then re-establish ties a month later as if nothing had happened. These days, I'll try to give a bit more context. Receiving a gift is not easy for me either, because I can't pretend to like something if I really don't. That stresses me out, but it also causes stress for my friends. Recently, someone suggested that I learn a few standard phrases to use when I receive a gift that doesn't meet my expectations.

Social contact wasn't always very easy. In my teens a friend once commented that she didn't always feel comfortable around me because she was afraid I'd make an inappropriate comment, and also because I always used difficult words. By difficult words she meant – you guessed it – that I liked to use words of Latin origin. But let's be honest, why would you say *hidden* when you could say *latent*? Or why say *shapeless* when *amorphous* is available to you?

Knowing myself better now, I can adjust here and there. But I remain who I am. I cannot change that person fundamentally (even if I wanted to). Too often I see people on the spectrum, especially those without a diagnosis, living in a state of uncertainty. Because you're supposed to be normal, you don't have a diagnosis, but you do behave different than everyone else.

Someone who didn't realize until later in life that he was on the autism spectrum is singer-songwriter David Byrne. In the 1970s and '80s, Byrne was frontman of the American rock band Talking Heads. Byrne was 57 when he first publicly announced that he *might* have a mild form of ASD, and more specifically what used to be called Asperger's, making him highly gifted, verbally articulate but socially inept. In various interviews he said that he now understands why he used to be so socially awkward, but also that he simply didn't realize it from his own perspective. In Byrne's case this insight unfortunately came a bit late, as his behaviour and egocentrism have effectively ruled out any future reunion of Talking Heads. The band broke up in 1991, apparently for good.

In the 2020 autobiography *Remain in Love,* Talking Heads drummer Chris Frantz writes about the early years of the band and how they amazed everyone with their innovative sound and striking music videos. He also talks about David Byrne, explaining that the group initially saw him as someone who acted weird. At parties, he would always isolate himself. He didn't dare look at people or would leave without saying hello. His social skills were awkward and unrefined, to say the least. An interesting and slightly spicy detail is that Byrne once told Chris Frantz that they needed a different bassist, despite the fact that Talking Heads bassist Tina Wymouth was Frantz's girlfriend, and is still his wife to this day. The autobiography also reveals that Byrne usually didn't participate in a conversation, but later captured the essence of that conversation in his song lyrics.

In my view, Byrne can count himself lucky that Frantz and Wymouth were not only the right musicians for the band, but also the right friends who tolerated his behaviour for many years. Until 1991, to be precise. Frantz has a nice description of Byrne's neurodivergence: 'He got into music to get out of himself.' And if you're still not convinced that Byrne is somewhere on the spectrum, there is also this testimony: 'He always made an unexpected move, both musically and physically.' I was a Talking Heads fan myself as a teenager, partly thanks to their absurd yet recognizable lyrics, such as 'strange but not a stranger'. I felt an immediate connection to the world of Byrne and his entourage.

The right friends are very important, whether you are on the left or right of the spectrum, as is a life partner who sees your way of being as unique rather than peculiar. Building a network of fans who can help you achieve your goals is what it's all about. For a young person still developing, a good mentor can also provide this context. A mentor could be an inspirational role model, or someone closer to home. For each condition, Part II therefore lists a number of well-known role models who can help you along the way. But you don't need to look that far. There may be people in your own life who are further towards the right on the spectrum and are making a difference professionally thanks to identifying and nurturing their own neurodivergence. Engage with them and learn from their life experiences.

# The importance of parents

As a ten-year-old, I played football every day on a plot of waste ground beside our house. Until pressure from friends and parents encouraged me to join the local football club. I went to training just the once. Back then, football was still a very static game and players only ran when they had the ball at their feet. I was a sprinter by nature and my running ability made me stand out from the start. After only one training session, I was invited to play an official match. The invitation sat on my parents' mantelpiece for weeks, but I never went back to the club. I still wonder why. As an individual I didn't feel part of the group, but I did feel responsible for winning or losing. I didn't want to bear that responsibility. Football, I see now, is not a fair sport: sometimes you get punished for things you don't do, others don't get punished for mistakes they do make, the game is a constant psychological battle. Team sports are not for me. Especially not football. I switched to athletics, which was more my thing. An individual sport, where I was responsible only for myself and my own winning or losing. And a fair sport, because if you win it's because you are better, and if you lose it's because the other person is better. A simple system. And as far as I'm concerned, a much better match for me. I'd like to thank my parents for not pushing me to give football a chance first. In that sense, I was lucky to have indulgent rather than authoritarian parents when it came to my choice of hobbies.

A nurturing context begins with the role of parents, who have a major influence on their child's self-image and development. This is not always an easy process: as the parent of a child with a diagnosis, you first need to go through a process of acceptance while people around you may still be making comments such as 'they'll grow out of it'. They won't grow out of it, they'll deal with it differently at different stages of their lives or it may be present to a greater or lesser degree at times, but neurodivergence is permanent. So for a parent, acceptance is a first step. And if you can then look at the positives it brings, the next step is embracing it. Observe your child, tolerate their weaknesses and identify and encourage their strengths. For example, it's only human to lose your temper with an ADHD child for not sitting still. Children with ADD lack the hyperactive trait, so there are no physical signs of a neurodivergent condition. These children deserve extra understanding, or you'll be quick to see them as poor listeners and daydreamers, forgetting everything even though you've just repeated yourself for the third time. They seem to lack awareness and not to care about anything. It helps if you know this is part of a condition. It also helps to know that, for every negative trait, there is a positive one. Try to find them in your child.

Providing a nurturing context as a parent is important for every condition in this book. Children with ADHD (and ADD) benefit from parents who are understanding but provide structure. In the same way, parents of children with ASD will be appreciated if dinner is always ready at a set time and activities are announced in advance, to mention something trivial yet essential. Children with dyslexia need the freedom to tackle things in their own way and want to be recognized and rewarded for their efforts. An understanding parent is a great help here. It also makes it easier to discuss the necessary support at school. Children with OCD also need a parent who is not too quick to criticize and allows them to express their feelings. Parents will need to sit down with their child and devise strategies to counteract their compulsive thinking or behaviour. This calls for a great deal of empathy.

The journey is long and demanding but, in the best scenario, it can be supremely satisfying. Like the moment when our son, at nine years old, abruptly said: 'Mum, Dad, I'm starting to believe in myself. As a baby I didn't believe in myself, but now I do.' That's what Noah told us recently during a car journey home. His words came out of the blue. And filled the car with a good feeling all round.

What if your child has mild symptoms and no diagnosis? Even then, a parent can make sure to name their 'difference' at the earliest stage, and if necessary seek guidance in order to maximize developmental opportunities. It comes down to discovering the talent and seeing if it can be transformed into a competency. A nurturing environment is crucial here. If you as a parent can compliment children on their talents, they will feel better, do things better, get better at something. The Cambridge University Press publication *The Psychology of Abilities, Competencies, and Expertise* refers to this as the 'multiplier effect'. A good environment acts as a multiplier for an innate talent. Our current education system still focuses on traditional talents, such as an aptitude for maths or language. But there are also other talents that deserve appreciation and support – spatial understanding for example, or a visual talent such as an extreme sense of colour, to name just two. Our system knows how to train a doctor or engineer, but all those other talents can also lead to surprising and distinctive competencies. As a parent, choose a school that has an inclusive perspective on talent.

With our son's diagnosis, it also became clear that a regular school education would not be feasible. He is currently in a type of special education for children with an autism spectrum disorder who have no intellectual disability but cannot attend regular education. Some features of this type of education have proved essential to him: smaller class sizes, noise-free chairs, focus corners, and so on. But even more important is the focus on the child's social well-being. The teachers pay great attention to maximizing the children's developmental opportunities. A gentle approach to difficult behaviour is needed in order to keep giving them those opportunities. As a parent, you always have a choice: either your child adapts to the environment, or the environment adapts to your child.

The impact of schools, and more specifically of teachers, is illustrated by the example of Louisa Bogaerts, a professor at Ghent University. The young Belgian researcher previously worked at the University of Amsterdam where she explored learning, language and memory. Despite having dyslexia, she was still able to study languages thanks to patient teachers and understanding parents. Towards the end of primary school a helpful teacher told her: 'Don't see it as a handicap, you can study anything.' Without that encouragement, she might not have become a professor with her own brain research lab.

# Don't make them fit in, help them stand out

## Are you a parent with your own condition?

You may be a parent of neuroatypical children. But what if you are neuroatypical too? As a neuroatypical parent, it's not always easy to raise your child when your own emotions sometimes tie you up in knots. In my own case, I know I run out of patience when I get overstimulated. I want everything to go as planned and everyone to act according to my own expectations. At times like these, I cannot call myself a good parent. Tempers can flare between me and my son (who, as you know by now, is on the autism spectrum himself). 'The clash of the autistics,' my wife always calls it. That description was very confronting for me, but it also opened my eyes. And changed my behaviour. I try not to get into confrontations with him any more. Now I use my own ASD to get a better sense of what is overstimulating my son and try to help him. It doesn't always work, but it sometimes does.

Towards the end of 2021, we went for lunch at B.O.U.L.O.M. in Paris' 18<sup>th</sup> arrondissement, a cosy buffet restaurant behind the façade of an artisan bakery. When we entered the restaurant, my son turned on his heel and went back outside. 'What's wrong with him now?', everyone wondered. I knew precisely what was wrong: the room was too big, there were too many people, the acoustics were an assault on the senses and they were going to seat us at a long table to be shared with another couple. What was wrong? That's what was wrong. Enough to not want to eat there. Luckily, the staff were understanding and found us an other available spot in a corner where it was quieter. Lunch could still go ahead.

As a parent, I now try to assess his feelings each time based on my own experience. This sometimes works, but by no means always, because everyone is at a different place on the spectrum and has different symptoms and different combinations with other conditions. So sometimes I get it completely wrong.

What I also do consciously is nurture my son's self-confidence. (And I should really do it more with my daughters too; I often catch myself believing I am dividing my attention evenly, but giving him a lot more care.) That self-confidence is very important to me, partly because every child needs it, but also because it's something I lacked in my own childhood. Besides nurturing his self-confidence, I also want to nurture his passions and join him in his quest for new interests. Without exaggerating, I've visited the Natural History Museum in Brussels at least seven times with my son because of his passion for dinosaurs. A family highlight was a visit to Copenhagen Zoo, where they had put twenty or so life-size dinosaurs in amongst the usual animals. While youngest daughter Lente had eyes mainly for the snowy owl, polar bear and tiger, Noah was looking for all the dinosaurs. I must say that I too was intrigued by the combination of real-life animals and realistic dinosaurs. In the gift shop, Noah wanted to find a Carnotaurus. The salesperson tried to assuage him with an Allosaurus or some other saurus, but Noah wasn't having that. He knew exactly which episode of *Jurassic World* on Netflix it had been in and passed this fact on to help the salesperson. After a long search, we found a picture of a Carnotaur among the finger puppets. Noah was happy. I was happy. Even the salesperson was happy. Noah's autism is very different from mine, but there are affinities as well, such as our love of language. I may have been a poor mirror for him at the start, but now I try to be a good one. And thanks to my own traits, an understanding and nurturing one as well.

## The right colleagues

When you start a project with someone, it helps to have someone who accepts you as you are, nurtures your strengths and compensates for your weaknesses. Your 'other half', in a sense. I am lucky that my wife complements and strengthens me, both as a life partner and as a work partner. This book would not have happened without her. Where I lose interest, she picks up the thread; where I find an anecdote, she sees structure; where I write, she rewrites. By the way, the chapters on dyslexia and OCD are all written by her; I just couldn't bring myself to delve so deeply into these conditions because they were less interesting to me. If only everyone could have a partner like her, in your personal and/or professional life, someone who provides your nurturing context, who understands you and balances you with complementary talents.

To make my point about the right colleagues, I'd like to zoom in on Tesla again. Not the car, but the inventor of the alternating current generator and other key components of the modern electricity network. Nikola Tesla was hailed as a great genius in his own time but was completely forgotten in the history books. The names we remember in the race for electricity are Thomas Edison and George Westinghouse. Tesla himself gained little fame from his pioneering work, and little wealth either. The reason lay not in his talent, but in his entourage. His path in life shows how important your work partners and colleagues are.

From the biography *Prodigal Genius: The Life of Nikola Tesla* by journalist John J. O'Neill, we can conclude that Tesla was incontrovertibly an unusual individual. The book contains enough first-hand anecdotes to suggest that his unusual behaviour can be traced to autism spectrum disorder on the one hand and obsessive-compulsive disorder on the other.

Several events in Tesla's life show that he liked to isolate himself. As a child attending mass, he preferred to sit away from the crowds in the bell chamber, and once he accidentally locked himself in a secluded chapel. At the height of his career, there was always a table specially reserved for him at New York's Waldorf-Astoria hotel. Preferably in an inconspicuous, out-of-the way place, according to O'Neill's biography. He was also convinced that being alone is the secret of invention; 'Be alone, that is when ideas are born'. Tesla was also extremely principled and rigid, other traits I would also link to ASD. They made him a gentleman, but also stood in the way of fame. For example, he refused an offer to share the Nobel Prize with Edison because he felt himself to be a discoverer of new playing fields and Edison merely an inventor within them. He did not believe the two were comparable. He also had an incredible eye for detail and could converse for hours, provided the topic was his pet subject of 'electricity'. In addition, he clearly had traits of OCD. His 'germophobia' appeals to the imagination: cutlery, handkerchiefs and other items had to be discarded after a single use. He also insisted on having his own toilet in the office. It is therefore clear that his talent needed to be protected and the right entourage would determine whether he would succeed.

Success and failure for Tesla depended on the people he surrounded himself with, and the extent to which they believed in and supported him. His first manager, US inventor Charles W. Batchelor, spotted Tesla's potential right away and introduced him to Thomas Edison. Batchelor was therefore a good match for Nikola Tesla and opened doors. Edison, on the other hand, turned out to be a negative experience: Tesla and Edison were intellectually on different wavelengths and had clashing values. Edison promised Tesla 50,000 US dollars if he could improve his dynamos, but failed to keep his promise, prompting the highly principled Tesla to resign with immediate effect. Luckily, his next encounter was another fruitful one. George Westinghouse and Tesla clicked right away. Westinghouse invested in alternating current, taking the fight to the supporters of direct current. Tesla's life continued in this vein, from good encounters to bad, from riches to rags, from success to failure, from star status to oblivion. He died alone in his New York hotel room on 7 January 1943. Tesla's story shows a clear pattern that makes the difference between success and failure. For Tesla to succeed, the bottom line was that he needed allies who met three conditions: (1) funding his experiments, (2) commercializing his inventions, and (3) believing in Nikola Tesla the person. In other words, the business instinct had to come from an ally, but that ally also had to have integrity and be supportive. After all, someone with ASD assumes that other people value honesty too, which is not always the case in reality. This is why I find Tesla's story so telling. In summary, choose your work partners carefully. They should take care of the business and social aspects, and should also be reliable, so the person with the special difference and corresponding gift can stay focused on the ideas and the work.

This is an illustration based on ASD, but there are also factors that contribute to the right match or mismatch for ADHD, dyslexia and OCD. Put two colleagues with ADHD together, for example, and they might well tire each other out and still not get anything done. Put two dyslexics together and their ideas might not get a platform, because they lack a colleague to put them down in writing. The right combination is therefore crucial. Here too, you may be on the left of the spectrum and have felt all along that certain colleagues suit you, but not others. Maybe there's just no neurological match? Earlier I mentioned my lecture *The power of neurodiversity* at the BAM Marketing Congress. After giving the lecture I noticed a growing realization among many attendees that they themselves or a colleague were somewhere on the spectrum. As people came up to me with personal questions, I overheard a conversation between two colleagues from Proximus, Belgium's largest telecoms company. It seemed they made a strong duo in the workplace, and they finally had an explanation for that: one of them was on the ADHD spectrum, the other on the OCD spectrum. 'We're a perfect match,' I heard them say, 'you start things and I finish them.' Do you want to know who you can form a perfect team with? At the end of the next chapter I will give a diagram showing which types of colleague can be your key to success.

# Chapter 13
# The influence of corporate culture

Not all that long ago, businesses were housed in vertical buildings and had equally vertical structures. Today those vertical buildings are still there, but inside them the structures are more and more horizontal. Welcome to a new world where values are becoming more important than rules. This is the positive influence of the new keywords inclusion and diversity, core values that are setting a new course for our society. This book is a plea to add neurodiversity to diversity. Neuroatypical people have just as much need for a nurturing and supportive culture. But why should businesses invest in a culture that also embraces neurodiversity? Because neurodiversity can be a competitive advantage for any business.

One of the first companies to implement a neurodiversity hiring program was Microsoft, followed by JP Morgan in 2015. Many other banks and tech companies have also adopted such programs, not only to improve their HR reputation but also to gain a competitive edge. In addition, the creative industry benefits from the unique skills of neurodivergent individuals. For example, it is often the case that the best designers are dyslexic and the best conceptual thinkers exhibit traits that could be considered autistic.

According to a report by the Deloitte Center for Integrated Research, teams that include neurodivergent professionals in certain roles can be up to 30% more productive and make fewer errors than teams without them. The authors refer to research conducted by Australia's Department of Human Services in collaboration with Hewlett Packard Enterprises. Rashmi Vikram, the Chief Equity Officer of the advertising agency Dentsu APAC, adds a word of caution, however, in an article in the global business magazine Campaign. She says, 'Attracting neurodivergent talent doesn't automatically mean we're hiring an individual of extraordinary capability. The savant syndrome, popularized by films like Rain Man and the recent South Korean drama Extraordinary Attorney Woo, creates an expectation from neurodivergent individuals that often only adds to the stress of navigating a workplace designed for neurotypical folk.'

Whatever talent they bring to the table, these special talents also have special needs. They bring something to the company, but the company should also bring something to them. Because they are vulnerable, several actions are needed to make them feel part of the team.

# Neurodiversity as a competitive advantage

Since COVID-19, each day brings a new situation that calls for new solutions. And just about everything needs to be rethought: new services, new payment methods, new products, a new HR policy. It helps if you have the innate talent to look at the world differently. There are, of course, books that teach you to think 'counterintuitively', such as Paul Arden's bestseller *Whatever You Think, Think the Opposite*. But if you're on the neurodivergent spectrum, 'Whatever You Think' is probably already the 'Opposite'.

In his book *Think Again,* author Adam Grant stresses the importance of keeping an open mind, as rapid change in every industry forces us to constantly review our norms and values. To support his argument, he kicks off with a gripping anecdote about a devastating 1949 forest fire in the US state of Montana, known as the Mann Gulch fire. A lightning strike had set the local forest ablaze and a special team of firefighters called 'smokejumpers' had been parachuted into the area to fight the fire. A sudden blow-up of the wildfire extinguished all remaining hope of getting the flames under control. But worse, the lives of the fifteen members of the smokejumper team were in danger. Foreman Wagner Dodge had an unorthodox stroke of inspiration that might just save his team's lives, an idea that, on the face of it, went against all logic. He called out to his team: 'Let's start a fire!' His solution was met with disbelief by his teammates, but finally he convinced them to start a fire of their own, burning out an area of forest and making it safe ground for the team. A variation on scorched earth tactics, in a sense. We don't know if Wagner Dodge had a form of ASD, ADHD or some other neurodivergence, but his unorthodox solution saved the lives of himself and two other team members. But what about the other twelve? Further research unearthed several articles showing that Dodge stood in isolation with his idea and couldn't convince the other team members to join in. This is important because it shows that unorthodox ideas are not enough in themselves, there needs to be a group culture or corporate culture of trust that will at least consider such ideas.

Many inventions and disruptive insights have been inspired by neurodivergent individuals who don't always prefer the familiar path. That alternative path usually doesn't seem safe, but it sure is extraordinary. This unorthodox thinking is what businesses need from anyone who deviates from the neurotypical, from the normal. More than that, it's what our planet needs. Drawing on the whole population and everyone's individual strengths creates more human resources, a wider pool of willing workers, more diversity of thought and more opportunities for innovation. Homogeneous groups of like-minded people seem comfortable at first glance. But heterogeneity will make for fundamentally better solutions. A football team isn't made up of eleven defenders. The most effective teams combine different talents and strengths. Diversity and inclusion will play an ever-greater role in the future. Being open to the needs of people with unique traits is the key to success.

# Recruiting differently

For people with a neurodivergent condition (whether diagnosed or not), an inclusive corporate culture is crucial. This starts during the recruitment process, which at some point should create space to discuss your specific needs. The process itself may also differ from that for a neurotypical person. For people with ASD traits, for example, the recruitment process should be made as predictable as possible and attach less importance to its 'social' aspect. Informal chats in the corridor or hypothetical situations involving role-playing are not a good barometer, and nor are face-to-face job interviews with interviewer and candidate looking each other straight in the eye, perhaps leading to uncomfortable situations. It's better to ask if you can take a test in the actual workplace. Interviews only reveal how well you can talk about a job; they don't tell the employer how you actually work. In addition, the job description will need to be very accurate so it matches your expectations from day to day. Many job descriptions are recycled or adapted from a generic template but, for people on the ASD spectrum, it is vital that as few words as possible are open to interpretation and that all tasks and responsibilities are clearly defined and delineated. The section describing working conditions will need an additional paragraph on physical conditions, such as 'our building is located on a quiet street' or 'your workplace is in an open-plan office, but you can work from home three days a week'. Your future employer will also have to look at your CV or résumé in a different way. On account of the difficulties described above (in yourself or due to lack of support), you may well have taken an atypical career course and not yet been able to show your full potential.

And, as an employer, don't ask for 'language skills' if language isn't required in order to do the job well. For some reason, language proficiency is still listed on résumés, even though it's not that important in many jobs. Being good at written language is often a relevant skill, especially in customer contacts, but even then you can rely on the help of spelling correctors or people around you. Stephanie Raber, advisor to the HOI Foundation focusing on dyslexia opportunities in the Netherlands, says: 'Spelling mistakes on a résumé can be off-putting, but recruiters could in fact take a kinder view. After all, they say nothing about the candidate's talent.'

Many people have doubts about being open about their neurodivergence during a recruitment process. Maybe that applies to you too. It's entirely understandable. You might not be sure if it will lead to suitable adjustments, or you may worry that your new colleagues won't understand or accept it. The decision whether to disclose your neurodivergence is a personal choice. Everyone has the freedom to choose to do so or not. You may think your position on the spectrum has little influence on your performance in the job, but for others it can make a world of difference. You may need to do less covering up and be more open and honest about what you find difficult. This can reduce anxiety and be very liberating. You may also be able to count on more support from managers and colleagues once they understand what makes you 'different', and you may feel less social pressure to develop friendships in the traditional way. More and more businesses now have special support programmes for people who have disclosed their neurodivergence. The COVID crisis has certainly contributed to this, as the line between work and private life became even more blurred and many neurodivergent people had no choice but to reveal their sensitivities. On the other hand, of course, it is also your right not to go public, if you choose not to be treated 'differently' from everyone else. Stereotyping is an age-old phenomenon, and it takes a lot of patience and dialogue to disseminate the right information. But all the same, try to assess whether the business has an open culture and if certain things can be taken into account.

Being open about my own mental disorder doesn't diminish my value and contributions as a scientist. Honestly, the truth feels like a second chance

Matt Kasson, mycologist

At the outset, it is useful to reflect on what you need to be able to give your best, and what you do or don't share with colleagues. Things that can help include sensory aids, such as an out-of-the-way office with low lighting or a soundproof room (useful for focusing), a noise-free office chair, dimmable lights, and so on. Or it could be a good framework in terms of planning and structure, so you can put your energy into your work rather than losing it needlessly to external factors. This is especially true for employees with traits of ADHD or dyslexia. For example, a desk in a corner can be useful for wandering off to a news website without feeling guilty, if it helps your concentration.

## Individual approach

You need an individual approach. Just because a particular spectrum is suspected, it doesn't mean that all of your needs are automatically known. But there are four areas that employers can take into account, according to the book *The Neurodiverse Workplace*:

→ *Difficulties with working memory*, which is the ability to retain verbal information for a short period. This can vary depending on your stress level and/or your level of anxiety. Difficulties with working memory can affect many areas, such as the organization and production of written work.

→ *Difficulties with 'executive functions'* such as planning, organization, structuring, prioritizing, focusing, remembering things, managing time and other self-regulatory skills.

→ *Difficulties with communication and differences in communication style.* You may have trouble understanding things, while others find it difficult to express their thoughts. Still others have trouble with various aspects of social communication (such as non-verbal communication or conversational skills) or with written communication. These differences in communication styles can affect your relationships at work, as well as your performance in the job itself.

→ *Many neurodivergent individuals have low self-confidence,* which can leave them feeling isolated, excluded, frustrated, 'different', depressed or anxious.

Raising awareness among team members and managers can be very helpful in teaching organizations to think inclusively in terms of neurodivergence and to take your individual needs into account as far as possible. This can avoid a lot of prejudice, frustration and discrimination. However, no two individuals with the same diagnosis have exactly the same needs. Nowadays there are non-profit organizations that hold special information sessions in the workplace in order to raise awareness. Especially in times of working from home, it can be useful to give information about the fact that all of that screenwork is especially tiring for some neurodivergent brains. Consider videocalls, for example, where interpreting body language and facial expressions poses an additional challenge. For 'normal' people too, by the way. On the other hand, working from home does offer the opportunity to work in isolation, provided the home workplace is suitably equipped and allows maximum focus. For several months I've been using a wooden cabin as an office. We have called it 'Teshima', which is not entirely coincidentally also the name of a remote Japanese island where no one can disturb you.

Inclusivity also extends beyond the workplace. For someone with characteristics of ASD, a company party will require much more energy due to the different processing of stimuli, leaving you with little energy to socialize in the end. Understanding on the part of your colleagues can avoid a lot of unnecessary stress. Maybe my big disappearing act could work for you too.

In the end, it comes down to creating as much psychological safety as possible, and that may take some time. Complete safety within a team is something that is built up slowly and takes patience, because you need to learn each other's user manual. Especially in these times where colleagues work remotely and are not always physically in the same place. We all have our prejudices that make us tend to simplify our world and divide people into boxes. And perhaps even to see other people in terms of absolutes. Only with time can this binary thinking evolve into a more nuanced and realistic view. In the grey zone in between, there is simply more room for dialogue. For example, I notice I do stay a bit longer at some office parties. If there's no loud music and you can hold a conversation, to my colleagues' surprise I'll sometimes stick around for a second glass.

# Office layout

An inclusive work culture also means considering the ideal office layout. Businesses have been on a constant quest for the perfect layout in recent decades. Many have opted for the open-plan office, but since COVID-19 we now work just as much from home. Endless column-inches have been devoted to the pros and cons of home workspaces and open-plan offices, but psychiatrist and author Theo Compernolle for one was happy to be rid of open-plan offices for a while. In his book *How to design brain-friendly flexible offices,* he argues that modern zoos are better for animals than modern offices are for people. A bold statement, but studies do indeed show that 90% of all employees dislike working in open-plan offices because there are too many distractions and too much noise. And that's when you survey people without a neurological condition. What about people with neurodivergence? You definitely don't want 'too many distractions' as a person with ADHD and you don't want 'too much noise' if you're on the autism spectrum. To give a comparison, my son's school puts tennis balls over the ends of the chair legs to ensure peace and quiet in the classroom. I'd have liked to have tennis balls on hand in open-plan offices too, not for the chair legs, but for the clicking keyboards, the chattering colleagues and the air conditioning that keeps breaking your concentration. In other words, forget open-plan offices. Not just to keep things bearable for your neurodivergent profiles, but also to keep up productivity for everyone in the business.

How do you know if it's quiet enough? In his book, Theo Compernolle says that 40dB is perfect, which is the quietness of a library. That is of course very quiet, so 50dB is okay too, which is the quietness – or should we now say the noise level – of a living room. Adding in smartphones and phone conversations takes us up to 70dB. That's already approaching the noise level at a busy road junction. The quietness of a library isn't feasible everywhere or all the time, of course, but you can make sure there are enough places where that 40-50dB norm is enforced. These make perfect reflection spaces for 'normal' people, but for people with ASD they are ideal for all activities. And you obviously need spaces where higher decibels are allowed; these are perfect for communication and collaboration. They may be more the right habitat for people with ADHD. In any case, every office needs a perfect symbiosis between the three functions of reflection, communication and collaboration. Make sure there are enough spaces that meet these needs and the needs of anyone with a neurodivergent condition. If space is limited, you can make an existing open office more sensory-friendly by using sound-absorbing partitions, converting a meeting room into a quiet space, or providing noise-cancelling headphones or earplugs.

# A final note on corporate culture

There are many different corporate cultures, so there are many options to choose from. A culture that is more individualistic will work well for someone with traits of ASD. You like to rely on yourself and prefer to avoid collective obligations. A culture that has strict standards and rules on working hours is good for someone with OCD. A person with ADHD traits may thrive in an informal culture where the social norms are not too strict. Whatever the case, it is essential for a neurodivergent person to land in a business that is open to diversity and inclusion, and pays special attention to specific guidance or support.

An inclusive culture will only catch on if it's not just something for minorities. It won't gain wider support unless it adds value for the majority as well. Many measures that make a work environment neuro-inclusive are actually good for everyone in the business.

This goes beyond the recruitment process. It's also about how people work together: with more focus on output and less on input. First of all, meetings can be made more inclusive by sharing agenda items in advance and factoring in enough time for quiet and reflection, ensuring that introverts too get a chance to speak. Second, clear rules and standards benefit everyone because they provide guidance and structure. Think about the unwritten rules in your organization as well, and how to make them explicit. Third, information can be shared differently, with visual support and clear language as a guideline. Raising awareness around neurodivergence can encourage people to communicate as precisely as possible, without using figurative language or verbal ballast. One way to start is by choosing a short and clear subject line for your emails. Besides all these functional aspects of the organization, think about the relational aspects of working together. Informal feedback and dialogue are a healthier basis than a one-off annual evaluation and help to optimize cooperation on an ongoing basis.

In short, a neuro-inclusive work environment makes working together more enjoyable for every brain and so for everyone.

# Human neurodiversity should be celebrated, not treated as a disorder

Devon MacEachron

# Conclusion

This is a book about hope. For my wife and myself, the hope that our son Noah (on the right of the spectrum) and our daughters Lente and Febe (on the left of the spectrum) will be happy and successful in what they do. The path is always more difficult when your brain works differently. But it *can* lead to excelling at something. We also hope that every reader of this book has discovered something extraordinary in themself or someone close to them. And that discovering these new gifts may lead to finding the right environment in which these newfound talents can come into their own.

To help you create the right context, the diagrams below list the main strengths for each condition, as well as the traits to look for in your colleagues in order to make up for your weaker aspects. You will also discover more about the right corporate culture for you, so you can make your invisible form of diversity more visible. After all, you have a lot to add in the world of today.

Hopefully you also found inspiration in our testimonies. We didn't choose the Einsteins of this world, that would be too easy, but they still give a sense that success is achievable even if your brain works differently. Anything is feasible, as long as you believe in it yourself. We come with a manual, but it's worth giving us a stage.

Between publication of the first Dutch edition of this book in September 2022 and this English edition, public interest in neurodivergence has soared. More and more employers are open to neurodivergent talents and some employment agencies even specialize in them. We welcome this trend and are pleased we can help to strengthen this wave of diversity and inclusion. Neurodiversity has been put on the map in the legal profession by the Belgian Legal Diversity and Inclusion Alliance and in the marketing sector by VIA Netherlands. We are also seeing lots of initiatives in the creative sector and we keep receiving invitations to give lectures. On publication of this edition, I was invited to speak at the Cannes Lions Festival of Creativity on the topic. We are grateful for these opportunities to continue spreading our message. What makes us happiest is the stream of responses from readers. Many have got to know themselves or their family members better and have been able to look at neurodiversity with fresh eyes.

Our brains are as unique as our fingerprints, so no one is really normal and no one is really abnormal either. If we focus more on everyone's strengths rather than just on correcting their weaknesses, we will be a richer society for it.

To everyone who feels different: hopefully from now on you won't just feel 10% different, but above all 100% special.

# Find your ideal colleagues and work culture

**ASD**

| Strength | Colleague | Culture |
|---|---|---|
| Perfectionist | Social | No social commitments |
| Systems thinker | Ethical | No open-plan offices |
| Problem-solver | Extraverted | Work From Home |

**ADHD**

| Strength | Colleague | Culture |
|---|---|---|
| Starters | Finishers | Extra challenges |
| Multitaskers | Organisers | No fixed working place |
| Entrepreneurial | Supportive | No fixed hours |

**DYSLEXIA**

| Strength | Colleague | Culture |
|---|---|---|
| Visual | Literate | No email culture |
| Holistic | Perfectionist | No procedures |
| Autonomous | Bridge builders | Stimulating self-confidence |

**OCD**

| Strength | Colleague | Culture |
|---|---|---|
| Passionate | Lighthearted | Life/work balance |
| Finisher | Sense of perspective | Appreciation for experts |
| Persistent | Boundary setting | Open minded |

# The whole
# is greater than
# the sum of
# its parts

Aristotle

# Epilogue

Emily Rammant here. I'd like to take over for this epilogue, in my capacity as a coach, but also as Peter's wife and the mother of our children.

As a coach, I am trained always to work holistically. That means I look for completeness in a person or team and aim to foster cooperation between forces that at first glance seem to work against each other. For me, it's the only way to experience the fullness of life. Our marriage too is built on this principle. Peter has an original outlook on life and surprises me every day with his creativity and powers of observation. I recently got rid of my bathroom scales because he can estimate my weight to within 100 grams. He knows better than I do where my birthmarks are on my body. He can predict when I'm about to be ill because my hair looks a little duller than usual. His different outlook makes him a master at reframing things. The subject matter of this book illustrates this nicely.

Peter thinks and reacts in different ways than I do. I find this enriching and it brings meaning to our relationship. Of course, his ASD traits do mean he is not always easy to live with. I know that his work colleagues sometimes find this as well. I recently administered an EQ assessment to gauge his emotional intelligence; it showed that he has a fairly low EQ of 78 (as with IQ, 100 is the average). In terms of IQ, on the other hand, he scores above average. On an emotional level, he lacks empathy, finds it hard to express emotions, inherently places little value on relationships (we often laugh at the fact that he only needs his own brain to keep him busy) and can sometimes show little flexibility in his thinking and behaviour.

Though he can still surprise me too. Somehow at times, all of these shortcomings can melt away like snow in the sun. Once you have a bond of trust with Peter and can see him when he's relaxed, your relationship is a safe cocoon where he *can* show empathy, talk about feelings and be surprisingly attentive to your well-being. For me, that's the best-kept secret of our relationship, and why I am still in love with him after more than ten years of marriage. This unconditional love also ensures that Peter continues to develop within our relationship, and to surprise me as a person.

It may sound rather romantic to see so many benefits in people with ASD. I am well aware that other variations of ASD can affect quality of life in a negative way. Our ten-year-old son has a more distinct form. He too has a cocoon where he can be warm and relaxed with people he trusts. But at the same time, he can be harsh to everyone outside it. This can be very painful, as I experienced myself when I was catapulted outside his circle of trust for three months after he had a bad dream about me. The manifestations were extreme: he refused to eat food I had made and walked around me in a wide berth for that whole period. Only with the right medication did these delusions go away and could I step back inside his cocoon. So I certainly recognize that ASD is a condition that poses its challenges throughout a person's life. But besides the challenges, every day I see evidence that much remains possible. And that, within the safe cocoon of our family, Noah can be a blissfully happy child with amazing imagination and creativity. He takes us with him on his journeys of discovery, making our world a little bigger in turn.

I hope that readers of this book who were triggered by the title have been able to discern certain behavioural patterns and character traits in themselves and experience moments of recognition, or even epiphany. That they felt something resonate in their own blueprint. This gaining of awareness, this light-bulb moment, is the path to personal growth. It is not by rejecting these traits but by accepting them that your full potential can be revealed. So I think it's worthwhile getting to know ourselves completely.

*'The whole is greater than the sum of its parts,'* as Aristotle taught us more than two millennia ago. He wasn't a Roman though, but a Greek, for which I apologize to my husband.

# Bibliography

Ahmed, Waqas (2018). The Polymath: Unlocking the Power of Human Versatility.

Arden, Paul (2006). Whatever You Think, Think the Opposite.

Armstrong, Thomas (2010). The power of neurodiversity: Unleashing the advantages of your differently wired brain.

Aurelius, Marcus (2003). Meditations. Translated by Gregory Hayes.

Baer, Lee (2016). Getting Control: Overcoming Your Obsessions and Compulsions.

Baron-Cohen, Simon (2022). The Pattern Seekers: A New Theory of Human Invention.

BDA (2015). 'Dyscalculia'. www.bdadyslexia.org.uk.

Bolen, Jean Shinoda (2014). Goddesses in Every Woman: Powerful Archetypes in Women's Lives.

Bolen, Jean Shinoda (1989). Gods in Every Man: Powerful Archetypes in Men's Lives.

Brakoulias, V., Starcevic, V., Sammut, P., Berle, D., Milicevic, D., Moses, K., et al. (2011). 'Obsessive-compulsive spectrum disorders: A comorbidity and family history perspective'. Australasian Psychiatry. 19 (2): 151–155.

Braun, Benjamin (2023). 'Neurodiversity in marketing: How my dyslexia helps me as a CMO'. www.campaignlive.co.uk

Buckingham, Marcus & Clifton, Donald O. (2001). 'Now, Discover Your Strengths'.

Chase, Chris (5 June 2014). The definitive guide to Rafael Nadal's 19 bizarre tennis rituals.

CIPD (Chartered Institute of Personnel and Development) (2018). 'Neurodiversity at Work.' www.cipd.co.uk.

Colvin, Geoffrey (2008). Talent is Overrated: What Really Separates World-Class Performers from Everybody Else.

Compernolle, Theo (2017). How to design brain-friendly flexible offices: Based on science, not on opinions.

Eide, Brock & Eide, Fernette (2011). The Dyslexic Advantage: Unlocking the hidden potential of the dyslexic brain.

Epstein, David (2019). Range: Why Generalists Triumph in a Specialized World.

Feinstein, Adam (2019). Autism Works: A Guide to Successful Employment across the Entire Spectrum.

Frankel, Miriam (2018). Nikola Tesla: The extraordinary life of a modern Prometheus.

Frantz, Chris (2020). Remain in Love. Talking Heads. Tom Tom Club. Tina.

Grant, Adam (2021). Think Again: The Power of Knowing What You Don't Know.

Grant, David (2017). That's the Way I Think: Dyslexia, Dyspraxia, ADHD and Dyscalculia Explained.

Honeybourne, Victoria (2020). The Neurodiverse Workplace.

Hofstede, Geert (2003). Culture's Consequences: Comparing Values, Behaviors, Institutions, and Organizations across Nations.

Howlin, P., Goode, S., Hutton, J. & Rutter, M. (2009). 'Savant skills in autism: Psychometric approaches and parental reports'. Philosophical Transactions of the Royal Society.

Jonkers, Aliëtte (2016). 'Onschuldige rituelen of dwangstoornis?' www.aliette-jonkers.nl/2016.

Joyce, James (1922), Ulysses.

Kahneman, Daniel (2011). Thinking, Fast and Slow.

Koren, Leonard (2008). Wabi-Sabi for Artists, Designers, Poets & Philosophers.

MacEachron, Devon (2018). 'Human Neurodiversity Should Be Celebrated, Not Treated as a Disorder'. Video published by NowThis News.

Marcellinus, Ammionus (2013). The Later Roman Empire: A.D. 354-378. Translated by Walter Hamilton.

Maxwell, John, C. (2007). Talent Is Never Enough: Discover the Choices That Will Take You Beyond Your Talent.

Meilleur, A. S., Jelenic, P. & Mottron, L. (2015). 'Prevalence of clinically and empirically defined talents and strengths in autism'. Journal of Autism and Developmental Disorders, 45.

National Autistic Society (2017). 'Autism facts and history'. www.autism.org.uk.

Nesse, Randolph M. (2020). Good Reasons for Bad Feelings.

NHS (National Health Services). (2016) 'Attention deficit hyperactivity disorder (ADHD)'. www.nhs.uk.

O'Neill, John J. (1944). Prodigal Genius: The Life of Nikola Tesla.

Oosterhoff, Menno (2021). Ik zie anders niks aan je: Over psychische aandoeningen en het brein.

Ozonoff, S., Dawson, G. & McPartland, J.C. (2015). A Parent's Guide to High-Functioning Autism Spectrum Disorder.

Ozturk, Alemsah (2015). Guide to Becoming Successful for People with Attention Disorder.

Perez, Caroline Criado (2019). Invisible women.

Quintilian (2002). The Orator's Education. Translated by D. A. Russell.

Reber, Deborah (2018). Differently Wired: Raising an Exceptional Child in a Conventional World.

Riedel, A. et al. (2016). 'Well Educated Unemployed – On Education, Employment and Comorbidities in Adults with High-Functioning Autism Spectrum Disorders in Germany'. Psychiatrische Praxis.

Salts, Gail (2017). The Power of Different: The Link Between Disorder and Genius.

Schippers, M.C. & Van Lange, P.A.M. (2005). 'The psychological benefits of superstitious rituals in top sport'.

Seneca, Lucius Annaeus (2018). Letters from a Stoic. Translated by Richard Mott Gumere.

Shaywitz, S.E. et al. (1998). 'Functional Disruption in the Organization of the Brain for Reading in Dyslexia'. Proceedings of the National Academy of Sciences 95.

Solomon, M., Miller, M., Taylor, S.L., Hinshaw, S. & Carter, C.S. (2012). 'Autism symptoms and internalising psychopathology in girls and boys with autism spectrum disorders'. Journal of Autism and Developmental Disorders.

Stein, J. Steven (2017). The EQ Leader: Installing passion, creating shared goals, and building meaningful organizations through emotional intelligence.

Sternberg, Robert J.& Grigorenko, Elana L. (2003). The Psychology of Abilities, Competencies, and Expertise.

Van Hoof, Elke (2021). Hoogsensitief. Wat je moet weten.

Vitruvius. Ten Books on Architecture. Translated by Morris Hicky Morgan.

World Health Organization. Regional Office for the Eastern Mediterranean. (2019). Attention deficit hyperactivity disorder (ADHD). https://apps.who.int/iris/handle/10665/364129

Zeidan J. et al (2022). Global prevalence of autism: A systematic review update. Autism Research. 15 (3).

**www.lannoo.com**

Translation: Sue Anderson
Design: Studio Lannoo
Photo of the authors: Jules August
Photo of Liesbeth Dillen: Vita June
Photo of Elise Cordaro: Leen Van den Meutter
Photo of Menno Oosterhoff: Hannah Radstake

© Uitgeverij Lannoo nv, 2023, Peter Ampe & Emily Rammant
D/2023/45/352 – ISBN 978 94 014 9507 3 – NUR 770